Tropicality
Houses by Andra Matin

Tropicality
Houses by Andra Matin

Foreword by Lyndon Neri
Text by David Hutama
Photography by Davy Linggar
With 275 illustrations

Contents

Foreword

Lyndon Neri

I first met Andra Matin about ten years ago when we were both invited to give a talk at the National Architectural Conference in Perth, Australia. Outwardly shy, Andra went on stage and gave a powerful hour-long lecture with his face turned away from the audience. No one seemed to care, however, as he tantalized them with a series of beautifully drawn diagrams, plans and sections that manifested into sensitive and beautiful projects. This was the beginning of a long friendship that has prompted me to visit him in Jakarta several times and allowed me to see in person many of the projects documented in this monograph.

To analyse Andra's projects and especially his houses, which are the focus of these pages, one needs to comprehend his ideas of home. Home and being at home are psychological constructs shaped by subjective perceptions of shelter, privacy, intimacy and a sense of security. Matin's houses serve not as mere containers and backdrops for life, but rather dwellings as expressions of values drawn from the most intimate planes of existence and from personal attachments. According to Heidegger, we build only after we are capable of dwelling; dwellings are the physical manifestations of our impulse to find rootedness in the world. Having had the honour and privilege of visiting Andra in his own home, I have experienced firsthand his deep commitment to this endeavour. While one might be tempted to draw connections and highlight similarities between the various residences in this book, I would argue that each one is its own unique quest to recover a certain primordial memory of 'home' — perhaps a memory of feeling protected, or of adventures in the garden, or of a rough texture against your skin. With each project, Andra brings his own distinct perspective and interpretation of dwelling that can't be encapsulated simply with terms like 'tropical modernism'.

In particular, Andra's masterful manipulation of both architecture and landscape, while it could be traced within a lineage of the region's vernacular typologies, is not as straightforward as one might think. Gaston Bachelard poses the house against the universe, where the power of dwelling is rooted in the notion of contrast, that its opposition to a general condition of a non-dwelling experience heightens its ability to reveal the dialectics of life: house–universe, interior–exterior, nature–artifice. While this dualism is certainly enhanced experientially, Andra does so by not drawing precise and defined boundaries. What is perceived as natural — for example, the grassy slope in the AM Residence — is actually a cleverly constructed topography to ground the architecture and re-establish interiority within the landscape. In the I&L Residence, it may seem that architecture is juxtaposed against nature, forced to concede to the existing palm trees, but what is truly remarkable is that ultimately tree and column are not only in harmony, they are at times indistinguishable from each other. This goes beyond familiar tropes of tropical buildings to redefine a contemporary architecture that speaks to Laugier's primitive hut, the ideal architectural form embodying what is natural and intrinsic.

Another aspect that stands out in Andra's oeuvre is the status he gives to non-space, or in-between space. Plato's concept of *khôra* comes to mind: an open space allowing for multiplicity, change and difference — alterity and alteration — it is concrete but also abyssal. In many of Andra's houses, whether inside or outside, there can be found undefined spaces whose function does not bear a traditional room designation such as 'living room' or 'bedroom'. Breaking through such conventions reflects a particularly astute understanding of human nature: that we need space to better discover ourselves where no prescribed role or function is given. The first floor of the AM Residence exemplifies this: upon arriving at this covered open area from the ramp below, one might not even realize they have entered the house, let alone the living and dining area, an open space that can equally serve convivial gatherings or tranquil solitude. The MA Residence is another that utilizes *khôra* to maximize the tight conditions of a compact site: angled volumes unfold, with voids cut from within to not only bring light and air, but to tie together the various spaces. A common thread in several projects is to reserve slivers of narrow space between the house and the site boundary; these seemingly leftover spaces, *khôra*, are actually critical buffer zones that allow the houses to breathe, to expand and contract as external conditions change — without them, the dwellings would remain stagnant and congested. For houses with larger sites like Omah Jati, Andra masterfully uses ramps, paths, landscape and the play of elevations to create intermediate spaces that bring about a seamless integration of his architecture with the natural environment.

Andra Matin's practice has always been modest. He does not seem to mind practising under the radar, as it were, mostly in his home country of Indonesia. I often take pride in telling people that his practice is the biggest secret in Southeast Asia, but given his recent and more public projects and the publication of this monograph showcasing 16 of his houses, Andra will no longer be inconspicuous. It is obvious that he is a gifted architect, and I am glad that our profession will start to take notice of the work of a great modernist in a country known mostly for its vernacular roots.

Introduction

David Hutama

Indonesian architect Andra Matin founded his firm andramatin in 1998, and in the ensuing decades has created an oeuvre that is both intriguing and aesthetically striking. In recent years, his work has gained an increasing amount of global acclaim: in 2022, Matin was honoured with the prestigious Aga Khan Award for Architecture in recognition of his design for the Banyuwangi International Airport in East Java. The award recognizes projects that enhance the quality of life in the Islamic world, and Matin is a most deserving recipient, his work serving as evidence of his commitment to designing buildings that are responsive to their context and beneficial to their users. His designs offer a distinct perspective on the integration of tropical elements in contemporary architectural design, blending tradition and innovation to create functional and visually appealing spaces.

The design of the airport exemplifies Matin's approach to tropical architecture, combining the traditional culture of Indonesia with modern design strategies. Notably, the roof, inspired by the traditional roof of the Osing house — a unique architectural style associated with the indigenous Osing people of Banyuwangi, East Java — demonstrates this fusion. It exemplifies the house's highly efficient passive design at a larger scale, with carefully designed openings, overhangs and landscaping that provide passive temperature control through natural ventilation and sun shading.

In 2018, Matin's *Elevation* installation received a Special Mention at the 16th International Architecture Exhibition of the Venice Architecture Biennale. The work was extraordinary on two levels: firstly, the geometry of a box of 5.5 x 6.6 x 6 metres enveloped on all sides by large panels of rattan weaving was a bold statement of simplicity among the works at the Arsenale; and secondly, within the box was a one-way 'Escher' staircase that mobilized visitors through a small but delightful exhibition of models of Indonesian vernacular architecture. These were displayed on varying levels of elevation that made the linear spatial sequence a playful spatial journey.

Elevation forms a miniature representation of how Matin perceives the architectural characteristics of his tropical archipelago. He frequently employs floating platforms, interplay of elevations and fluid dialogue between the landscape and interior space through dynamic spatial sequences to absorb the tropicality of the location.

But what is tropicality? The term has been a long-discussed yet uncontested topic across Southeast Asia. The catalogue of the exhibition Tropicality: Revisited — Recent Approaches by Indonesian Architects, held at the Deutsches Architekturmuseum in 2015 and 2016, describes tropicality as not merely responsive to climate or topography, but also about the identity of a place:

'For the last 50 years, Indonesian architectural discourse seems to hover around ... the problematization of identity. For Indonesian architects, identity and tropicality have never been a conquered territory. Like a pair of ghosts from the past, the two go hand in hand and constantly reappear in discussions among architects and the general public. Identity comes as an imagination, a projection of our own shadow filled up with reflections and our longings. Architectural identity precedes commissions, infuses ideals before an architect's drawing tables.' (PAGE 13)

On that account, representing the architecture of this region with an exotic tone tends to be the classic narrative; the terms 'regional' and 'vernacular' are typically discussed in relation to tropical buildings, but rather than learn from the wisdom of this architecture, there is a tendency to glorify particular forms or ornamentations.

Matin, by contrast, empowers tropicality by refraining from glorifying identity through these divisive gestures. Rather, he presents tropicality as a design approach that is extracted from various building practices in the archipelago. The place itself — nature, climate, geography and topography — defines the fundamental constraints and at the same time provides invaluable opportunities for place-making. Hence, Matin does not perceive these aspects as obstacles. His architecture is an embodiment of what might be termed a playful approach amid the complex discussions.

This optimistic standpoint positions Matin's architecture as an alternative resolution. Tropical architecture needs neither rich and exotic decorations nor ornamentations that represent a particular place or ethnicity; it also requires no festive materials. For Matin, the key to playing with tropicality is the site's sensibility, allowing occurrences of dialogue between the building mass and the landscape. By honing this exterior–interior interaction as the main strategy, Matin moulds the space and directs the spatial sequences. The form of the building appears as if it only functions as a vessel or a frame to facilitate the curated spatial experiences. Therefore, on entering one of his residential works, one might begin to feel as if the building was receding, allowing the voice of the site to speak louder than the architecture itself.

Embracing this version of tropicality, Matin's work seamlessly weaves together design elements sourced from the archipelago's diverse architectural practices, sidestepping divisive identity emphases. Nature's significance, climate's influence, geographical factors and topographical intricacies all shape his place-making endeavours. Notably, though, the spatial arrangement of traditional Balinese houses significantly informs his own spatial orchestration: Balinese architectural tradition treats specific functions uniquely, resulting in a fragmented spatial composition, and Matin views this detachment not as a flaw but as a wellspring of traditional wisdom, facilitating an adaptive spatial layout suited to the humid, rain-soaked conditions of the tropical region.

Presenting 16 of Matin's residential creations completed between 2006 and 2023, this book depicts the way the architect artfully harnesses tropicality to infuse everyday existence. Beyond grand concepts, his designs unfold elegantly, showcasing how the allure of the tropics can harmonize with the spatial efficiency of modern architectural approaches. These projects offer a glimpse into Matin's acute sensitivity to landscapes and their surroundings, an integral facet of his journey to assimilate tropicality into his architectural tapestry.

Projects

Andra Matin

Jakarta, 2006

WH Residence

First Floor

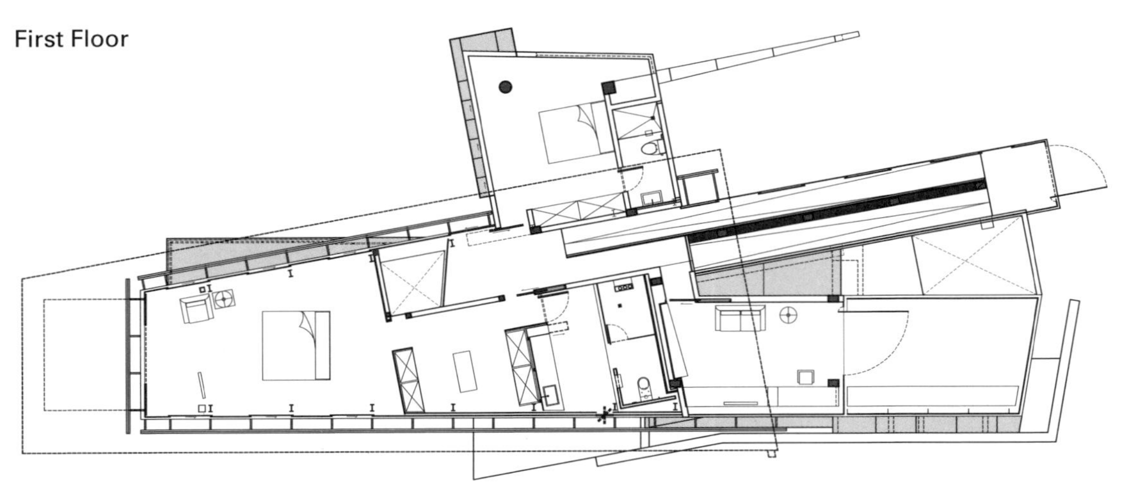

Ground Floor

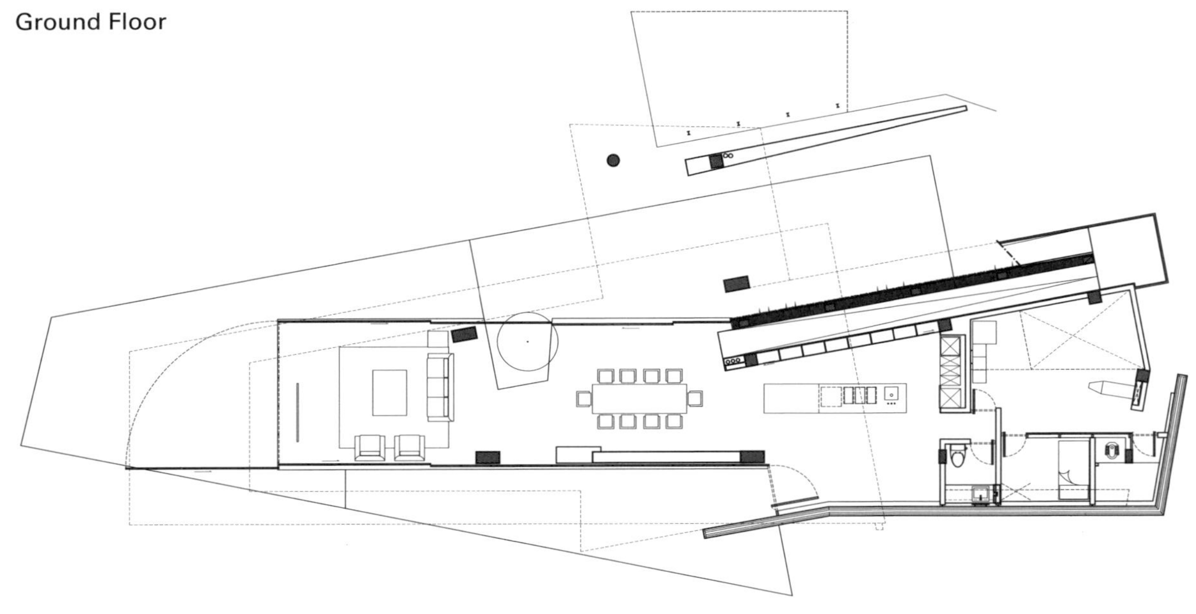

This residence stands as a testament to familial ties, situated on the property of the family's matriarch and providing a warm, tranquil gathering space. Reflecting the dynamic lifestyle of its inhabitant, an entrepreneur, the design radiates playfulness through angular compositions, elevated structures and an intriguing interplay between interior and exterior spaces.

The essence of the concept stems from the notion of crafting an efficient tropical dwelling that eschews the need for air conditioning, and this guides material and spatial choices; in fact, the living room transforms into an open terrace by allowing all enclosed walls to open up when conditions are amenable.

Comprising two interconnected boxes, the dwelling showcases the fulfilment of the brief through a dichotomous approach: the southern box emanates a robust aesthetic, achieved with GRC panels, while its northern counterpart exudes warmth and lightness, adorned with timber panels as secondary skins that amplify its personality.

Matin and his team gave meticulous thought to the strategic positioning of the building within its 800-square-metre plot, ensuring a visually pleasing and harmonious overall massing. On approaching the structure from the courtyard, attention is naturally drawn towards a grey box aligned along the north–south axis, a defining feature of the front elevation despite its narrow width of 3.5 metres. Employing a box-in-box approach, the design deftly organizes the interior space and slab orientation, facilitating a seamless transition between the ground and first floors.

The ground floor comprises a semi-public area designed for shared meals and social gatherings. The dining room takes centre stage, flanked by the pantry to the north and the living room to the south. The northern part also holds the service spaces, such as bathrooms, a helper's room and a drying area.

The first floor is home to two private bedrooms: a master bedroom and a guest bedroom. The master is an impressive sight, enhanced by a seven-metre cantilever structure that supports and extends it over the northern side. This innovative feature adds dynamism and elegance, but beyond that it maximizes the use of the available area as well as allowing for unobstructed views and abundant natural light, forging a seamless connection between the interior and the surrounding environment. To the north, a study continues this motif, providing access to a wooden roof deck.

A further remarkable feature of the design is the U-shaped ramp that connects the two levels. Unlike conventional stairs, the ramp serves as a vertical connector, enhancing the overall spatial experience. Its gentle slope facilitates a smooth transition between levels, inviting occupants to appreciate the changing elevation at a leisurely pace, as well as ensuring greater accessibility and convenience.

AM Residence

Roof

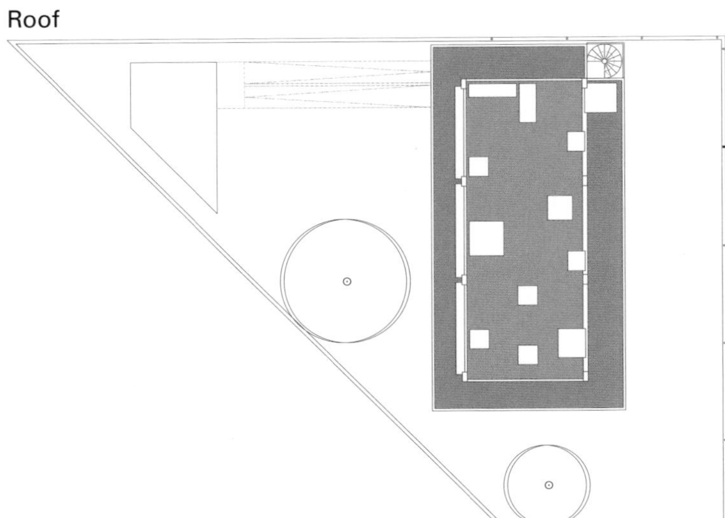

Second Floor

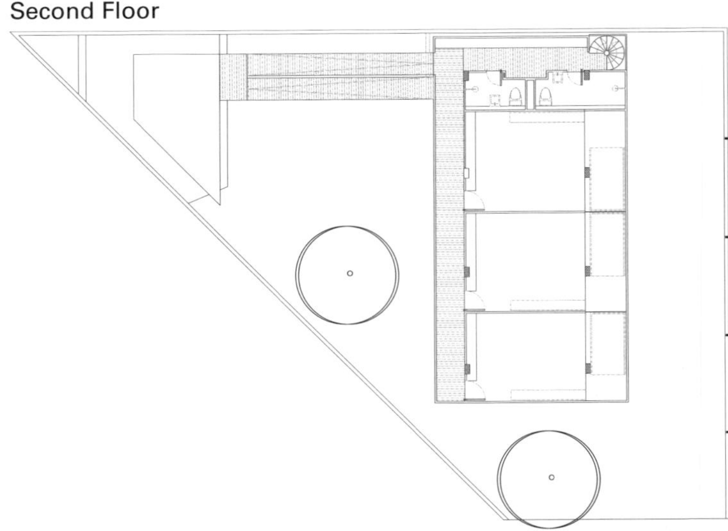

First Floor

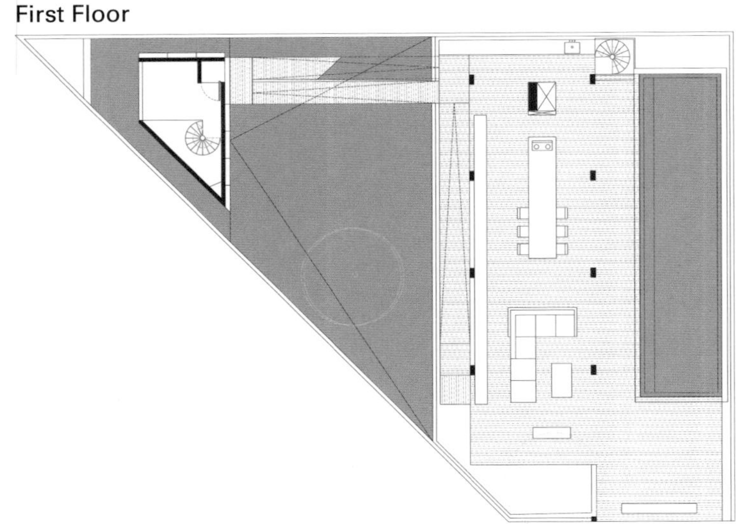

Ground Floor

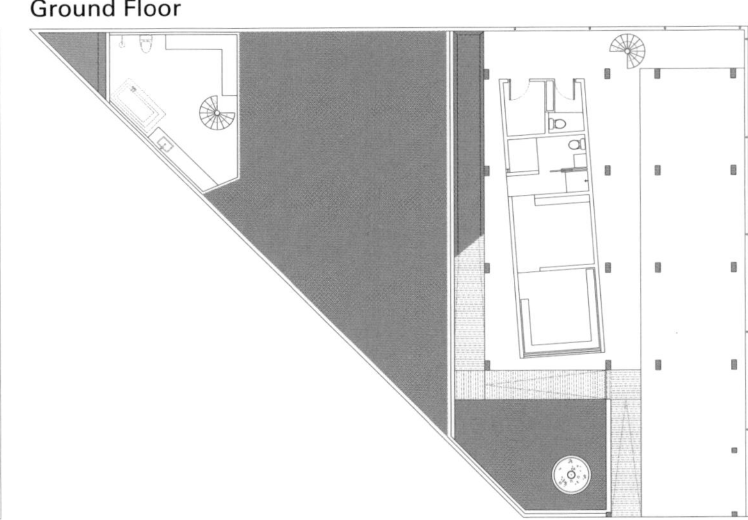

The AM Residence, which houses an architect, his wife and their three children, is situated on a triangular corner of land within a charming residential area in South Jakarta. Given the site's unusual shape and its positioning between two other houses, adopting a creative and unconventional approach was imperative.

The owner's fondness for the neighbourhood stems from its central location and adjacent park. Drawing inspiration from this, Matin envisioned a house that seamlessly integrates with its green environs. A *trembesi* tree at the centre of the inner courtyard formed a primary element in the spatial composition, with the owner wanting to see it from his bedroom.

Entering the AM Residence is a spatial journey in itself. On passing through the gate, visitors encounter a fishpond and a library. The journey continues along an elbow-shaped ramp that connects the street level to the elevated ground floor. Walking along this ramp feels like transitioning from below ground to a bright and expansive space, with the transformation from dimness to openness truly captivating.

The living room is key to the scheme. Elevated to provide a direct view of the park, it functions as a floating platform, supported by pilotis, on an elevated ground level supported by building up land adjacent to the main structure. This elevated ground floor extends the room, dispelling any apprehension of a cramped and dim space. The design choice not only introduces sunlight and fresh air but also opens the space, offering a welcoming, airy ambience.

The house is thoughtfully designed as a compound of spaces, with programmes strategically dispersed rather than enclosed within a single mass and each zone demonstrating its own characteristics. This fragmentation creates a rich spatial experience in what is a relatively small space, with every programme enclosed in a very simple geometry.

The living room platform becomes the home's main mass, with the level below serving as a garage, service area and library and the level above home to the children's rooms. The level stretches from the ramp entrance to the opposite wall, complementing the living room with an elongated swimming pool. The children's rooms above are equally exceptional, connected by a common space that acts as a hub, themselves resembling Japanese capsule hotel rooms and extending along the length of the box.

The positioning of the master bedroom separately at the back corner of the plot is part of Matin's strategy to maintain the inner courtyard as the main anchor. This second mass is accessible via a ramp from the main building, housed in a box-like structure whose lower level is enveloped by the built-up land. Its entrance is situated on the upper part of the structure, while the lower level serves as the bathroom. This open quality that seemingly replicates the neighbourhood park inside the property somehow transforms the house into a sort of communal space.

Opening the door to the master quarters, one is struck by the bedroom's placement on the corner side of the triangular box. To the left, a spiral stair connects the sleeping space to the bathroom below. The positioning of this buried space creates a unique ambience, with sunlight streaming in through an opening in the corner, adding a further compelling touch to the master bedroom's — and indeed the home's — spatial journey.

IT Residence

Section

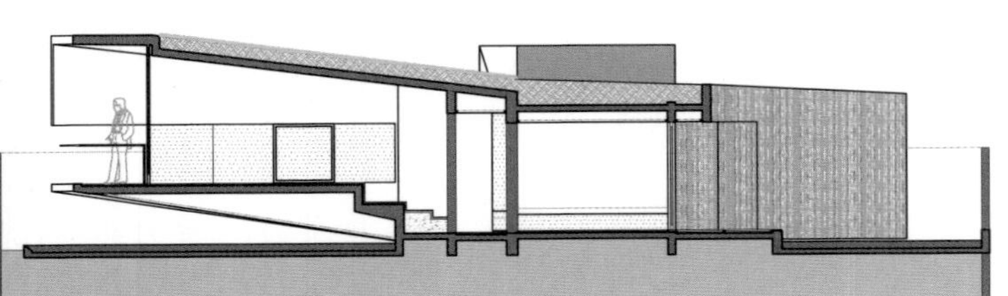

Ground Floor

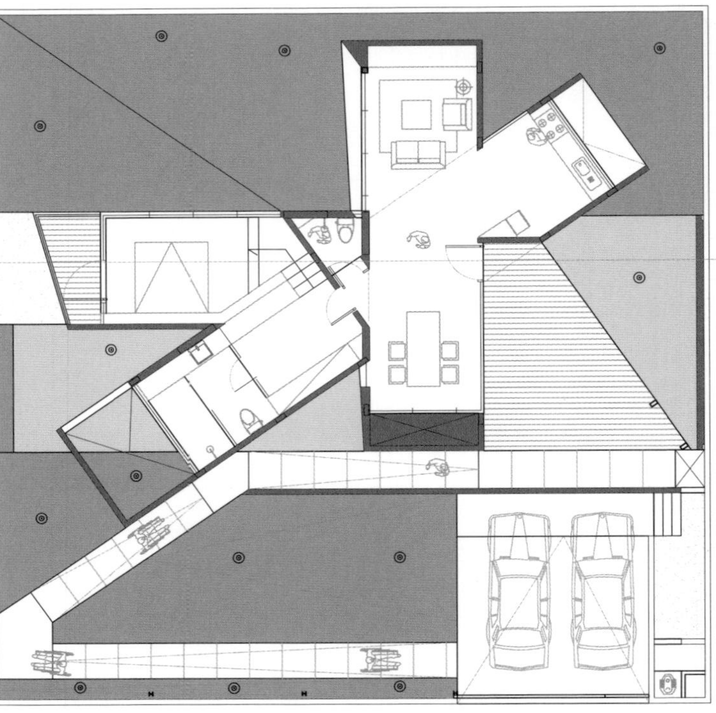

This project in the West Java city of Bogor came from a stroke of serendipity. The owner was well advanced in the process of building a new house, but wasn't entirely satisfied and felt that a second opinion might be beneficial. When he approached Matin for his input, the project was almost complete, and after a tour, Matin pointed out that improving the home's flaws through renovations would be challenging given that the structure was already fixed and the spatial composition established. The owner took his advice, and decided to redesign from the ground up.

Despite its modest size, the home creates an atmosphere of spaciousness and warmth. Positioned with its long side facing the road, the rectangular structure welcomes visitors through a well-designed main entrance on the eastern side that seamlessly connects the interior and exterior spaces. Indeed, from the moment one sets foot on the property, its harmonious integration with the natural surroundings becomes evident.

The massing of the house, characterized by concrete boxes adorned with timber finishes, achieves a modern yet rustic sculptural expression. By purposefully avoiding excessive articulation, Matin ensures that the architectural expression harmonizes with the open space, working within its compact area without overpowering it.

The home's entrance is accessed via a captivating U-shaped ramp that not only serves a functional purpose but also engages the senses, gradually unveiling the architectural design. Ascending the ramp evokes a sense of anticipation and discovery, a signature approach employed by Matin.

Inside, the living space is arranged symmetrically, comprising three interconnected rectangles overlaid on each other at an angle. Typically, employing rooms with a width of five metres in a rectangular shape may make an interior space feel stretched and linear, potentially inducing a sense of confinement. Here, though, the main rectangle and the diagonal rectangle that intersects it utilize clever perspectives, partitions and floor levelling techniques to manipulate visibility and create an illusion of expanded interior space. Matin also avoids fully enclosed spaces, mitigating any claustrophobia and instead fostering a playful and tranquil environment. The design moreover allows each room to establish its own unique connection with the surrounding yards, providing an engaging experience for the occupants.

With regard to zoning, the main bedroom occupies the southern part of the house, while the living room area is situated in the northern section, allowing for privacy and a clear separation between public and private spaces. Notably, the bedroom's floating massing stands out as a striking feature, creating an overhang that forms a pocket space underneath — a cool and serene spot for relaxation. In this space, one can enjoy the feeling of being on an island, surrounded by lush greenery and timber boxes, all while being surprisingly close to the street.

AS Residence

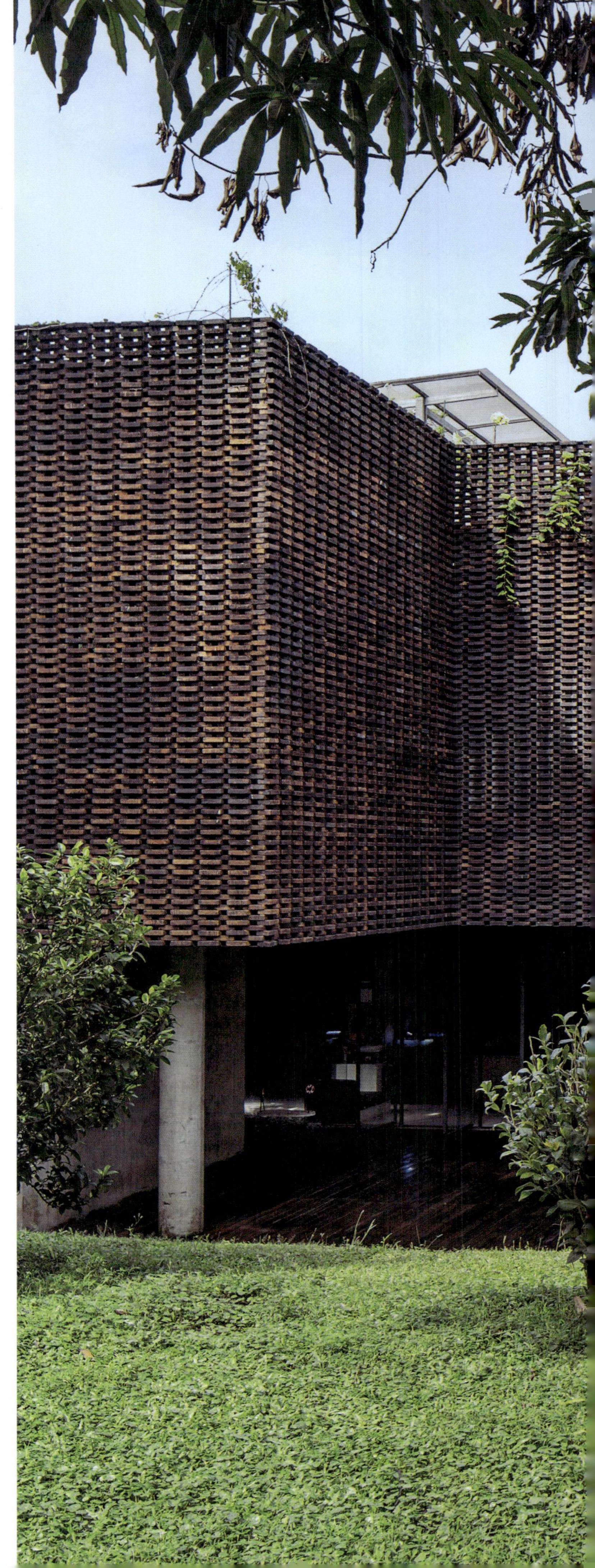

Roof

First Floor

Ground Floor

The AS Residence is situated within the vibrant confines of Yogyakarta's southern *alun-alun* (square). This culturally rich city, known colloquially as Jogja, is a bastion of Javanese art and intellectual pursuits, offers access to natural beauty such as Mount Merapi, and boasts iconic heritage sites such as the Borobudur and Prambanan temples.

Prior to embarking on the project, the owner (a painter) had opted for a lifestyle with his living quarters distinct from his workshop, in the belief that separating work and personal spaces would contribute to a more balanced existence. However, the arrangement had proven counterproductive, as he grappled with thoughts of family and household that hindered his productivity. Consequently, a new approach beckoned: integrating his abode within the workshop complex itself.

In relaying his vision to Matin for the project, the owner underlined the paramount need for privacy. Given the proximity of the new residence to his workshop, he aimed to establish a clear demarcation between the two realms; the flow of workshop visitors could not encroach on his family life or intrude on his personal time. From this, it was decided to create a three-bedroom dwelling ensconced in an enclosed space. A creative dimension also emerged, as the painter expressed a desire to incorporate local bricks as a pivotal architectural motif — specifically, he desired black bricks, inspired by a sighting during his travels.

The site acts as an extension of the existing workshop, with the prevailing wind direction from the rear to the front; consequently, Matin decided to sink the house while elevating the workshop building. This arrangement fosters dynamic interaction between the two structures and their respective activities, while a courtyard situated between them mediates and facilitates their dialogue.

Embracing an introverted architectural ethos, the residence forgoes the conventional street-facing facade. Instead, it embraces a design characterized by a box structure adorned with a secondary skin of the sleek black bricks. This discerning choice yields pronounced benefits, particularly within Yogyakarta's tropical climate. Bricks, renowned for their remarkable thermal properties, adeptly absorb and disperse heat. Here, the arrangement forming this secondary layer emerges as a natural insulator, skilfully regulating the interior temperature of the dwelling. And beyond their thermal prowess, the brick walls double as shading mechanisms, minimizing heat infiltration and curtailing the necessity for excessive air conditioning usage. In terms of aesthetics, Matin's innovative installation presents the bricks as floating in the air, achieved by suspending them using steel rods.

Moreover, incorporating local bricks as the key architectural element seamlessly blends traditional material into a contemporary context. The use of black bricks imparts authenticity and cultural connection, reflecting the painter's commitment to sustainability and practicality in Yogyakarta's climate. The AS Residence stands as a captivating and enchanting abode in the heart of this vibrant city, enriched by Yogyakarta's blend of cultural heritage, intellectual pursuits, natural beauty and royal traditions.

Bandung, 2013

EH Residence

Section

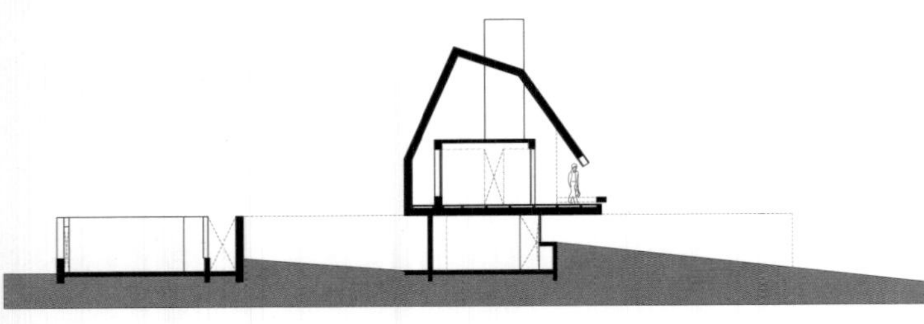

Elevation

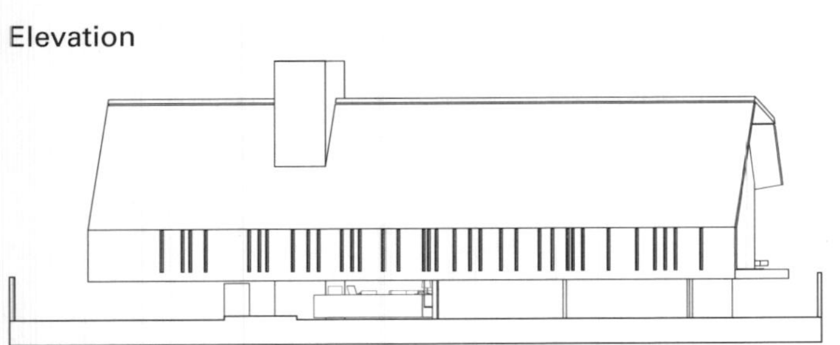

First Floor

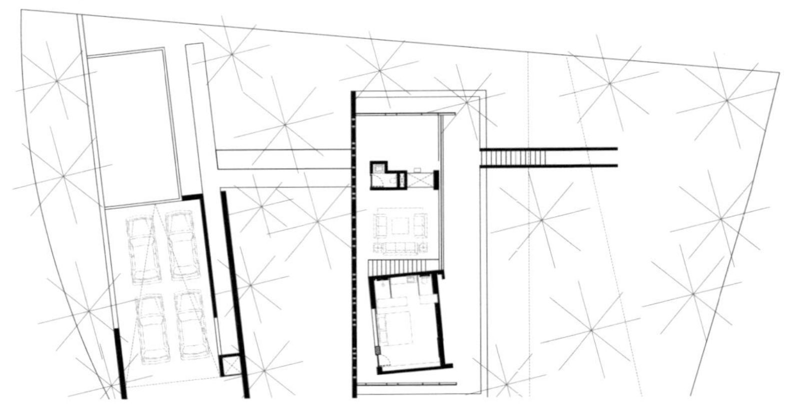

Ground Floor

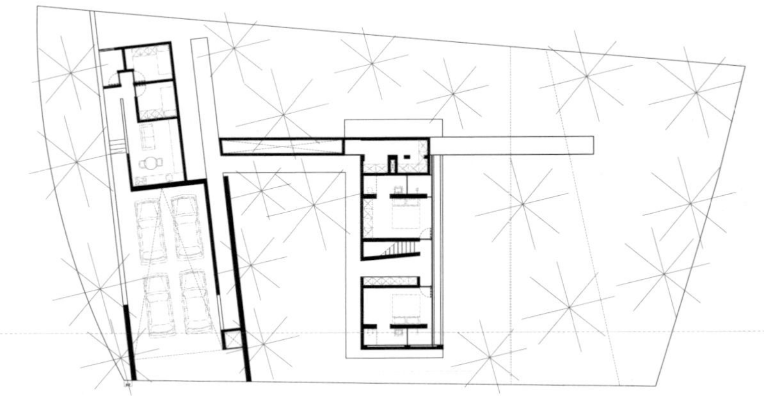

The city of Bandung boasts a reputation for captivating vistas, temperate climate, and rich historical and cultural heritage. Enveloped by verdant hills and idyllic landscapes, the city offers an escape from the typical urban life. Its architectural panorama showcases a captivating interplay between colonial-era structures and contemporary designs, resulting in a tapestry of architectural diversity.

Against this backdrop, the EH Residence commands attention, a prominent presence in northern Bandung's elevated terrain, offering panoramic city views despite the constraints of limited space. Here, Matin embarked on a strategic journey, navigating the contours of the compact land to optimize the points of visibility. Shifting the emphasis from external mass, he ingeniously inverted the approach, crafting expansive, cocooned interior spaces, nurturing a dynamic interplay between indoor and outdoor realms while fostering an atmosphere of playfulness and harmony.

Marking the third residence within the client's architectural journey with Matin, this house embraces a robust tropical vernacular, where a sprawling, expansive roof emerges as the defining architectural motif, deftly addressing the tropical region's considerable rainfall.

The project seamlessly melds with its verdant surroundings, cloaked in a lush canopy of trees, revealing only its prominent mansard roof from the exterior, representing a departure from traditional facades. Through a minimalist material palette — largely timber and concrete — and Matin's innovative box-in-box strategy, the EH Residence forges an outwards-looking spatial narrative, providing a conduit to engage with the marvels of nature. Unique in its approach, the entrance deliberately avoids a direct route to the house, while the site's ambiguous orientation bestows an element of architectural camouflage. An enclosed U-turn corridor ushers visitors through, leading to basement bedrooms via a suspended ascent. Progressing upwards, a platform unfolds, offering an unobstructed vista of the picturesque valley.

From here, the site's thoughtful partitioning into three distinct zones can be seen: the welcoming foyer, the heart of the house and the serene backyard. While the foyer encompasses a modest carport and entryway, the overall design leans towards introversion: the facade, intentionally concealed from the road by trees, envelops the house in a cloak of privacy and seclusion. This nurtures a profound connection between the interior and its occupants, fostering a tranquil atmosphere insulated from external clamour and distractions.

Behind the discreet facade, the EH Residence unveils expansive, well-crafted interiors that prioritize openness and interplay between indoors and outdoors. Serving as a massive canopy, the house's roof is supported by two Y-shaped timber structures on its edges, mimicking the function of an umbrella in providing shelter to all activities beneath while remaining detached. Teak graces the interior while ironwood adorns the exterior, resulting in a harmonious blend of materials.

Matin's design choices allow the inhabitants to fully immerse themselves in the interior environment while embracing the surrounding natural beauty. The introverted facade approach establishes a unique identity that sets the EH Residence apart from its context. It challenges the conventional notion of facades as mere visual representations and instead focuses on cultivating a tranquil living environment that nurtures a profound connection between inhabitants and their immediate surroundings.

Unique elements aside, the choice of the mansard roof is particularly intriguing as it resonates with Bandung's architectural heritage, especially prevalent among colonial houses in the city. But beyond its contextual relevance, the style creates additional interior space within the roof structure, allowing for more usable areas or attic rooms. It also promotes superior air circulation and temperature regulation within the building, providing a benefit in the tropical climate.

Bandung, 2015

IH Residence

First Floor

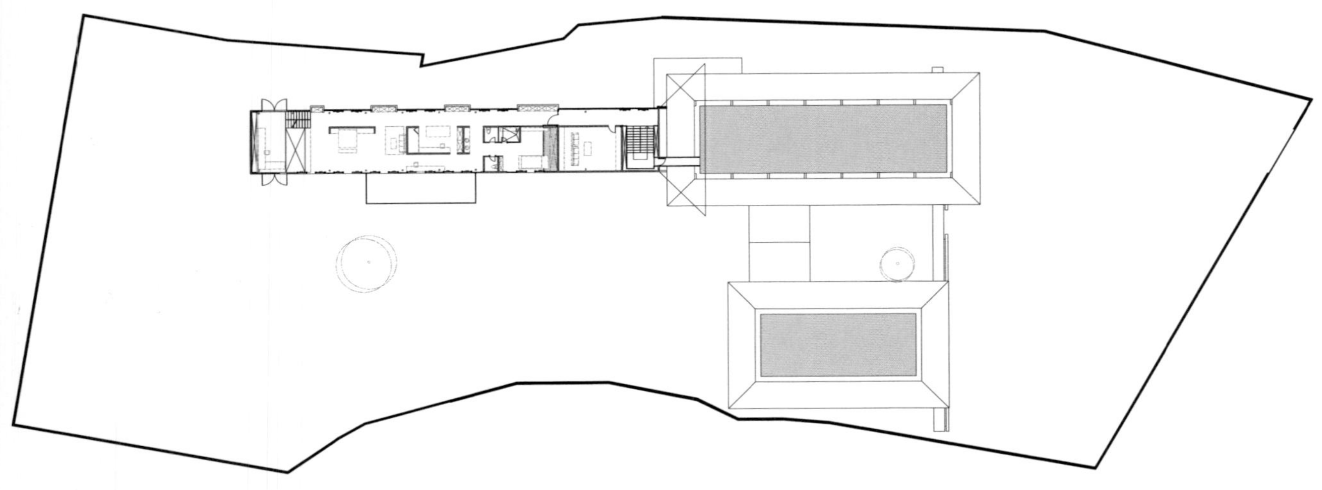

Ground Floor

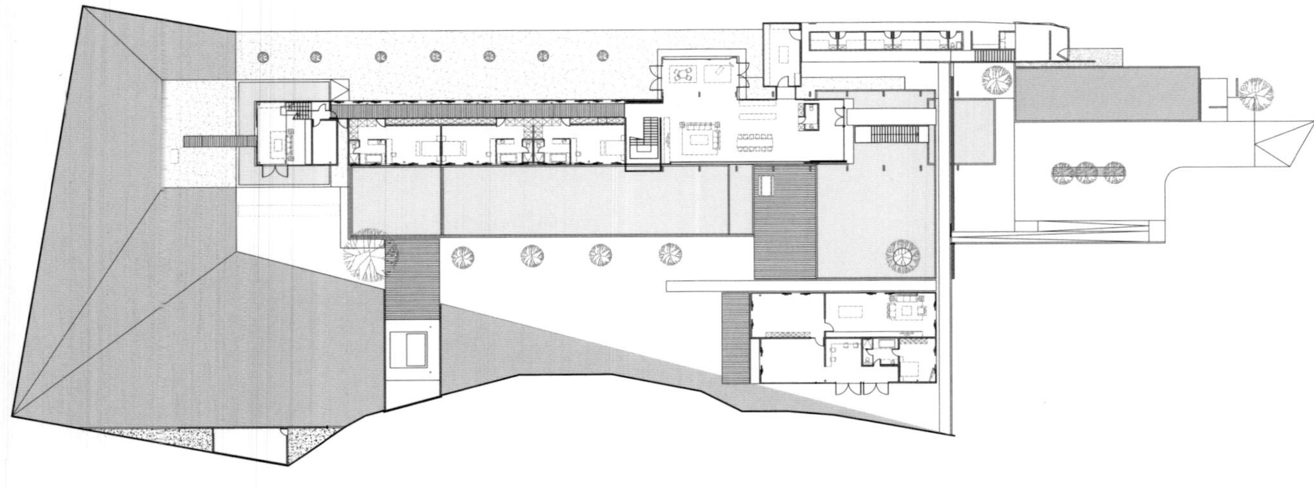

Basement

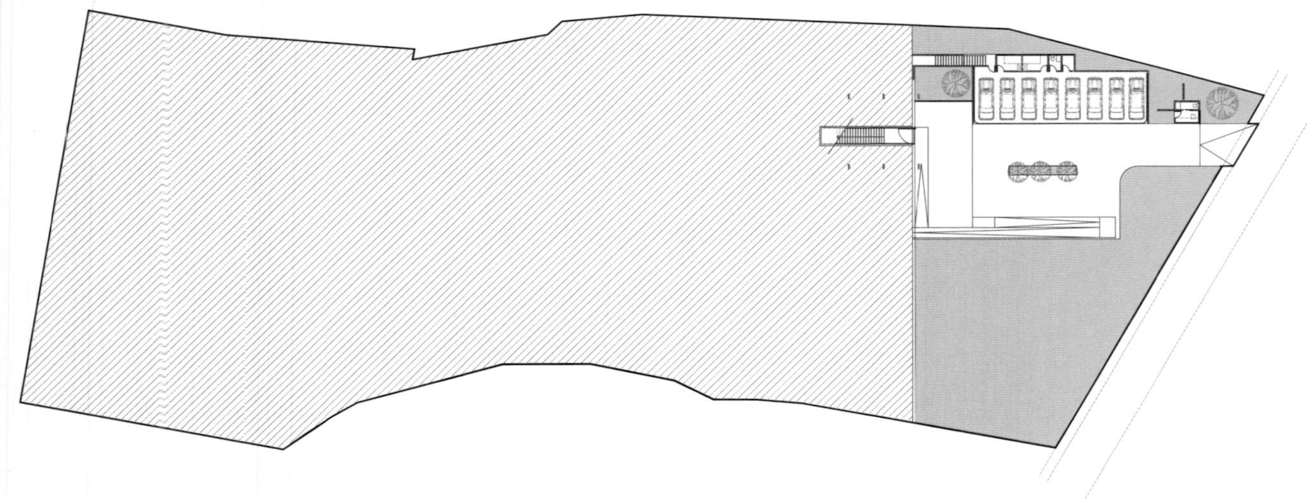

The IH Residence boasts a striking architectural feature — an expansive roof supported by pilotis — recurring in Matin's designs. This gesture exemplifies the architect's embrace of the tropical context, responding ingeniously to the Bandung region's constant heat and high humidity. Functioning much like an umbrella, the roof reflects a vernacular design approach tailored to the context.

Simplicity characterizes the massing, comprised of two box-like structures thoughtfully oriented towards the centre to prioritize views and a connection to the surrounding landscape; the approach harmonizes the architecture with the natural spectacle without overpowering it. Acting as pavilions, the structures offer unique views and easy access to the landscape, ensuring optimal air circulation throughout.

Predominantly constructed from concrete and timber, the pavilions exude both durability and warmth. Transparent glass partitions facilitate practicality while seamlessly connecting the interior and exterior, and the limited material palette aids in blurring the boundaries between nature and the man-made structure, harmonizing the architecture with its surroundings.

The project's generous land area also presented an opportunity for innovative site planning. To balance its spacious outdoor environments with a cohesive architectural composition, Matin paid close attention to the organization of programmes.

The strategic location of the main entrance on the northern side, accessed via a long ramp, creates a sense of spatial suspension, guiding visitors towards the heart of the compound. At the pinnacle of the main pavilion lies the master bedroom, providing the best range of visibility while ensuring utmost privacy.

Spatial boundaries are subtly defined, but give visibility to the transition from semi-private to private areas. The shift from paving blocks to lush grass, for example, signifies the transition from a semi-private area to the private domain of the house. Beyond this point, visitors' movements are confined, though the sense of freedom remains.

An inner courtyard acts as an oasis amid the city, integrating interior and exterior. Acting as a natural airflow pathway, it also enhances cross-ventilation within the living spaces, reducing humidity levels and promoting a refreshing environment. It provides abundant natural light to the interior, while itself offering an intimate outdoor space for relaxation and connection with nature. Whether for gatherings or solace, the courtyard elevates the living experience, bridging the tropical environment and a comfortable indoor ambience.

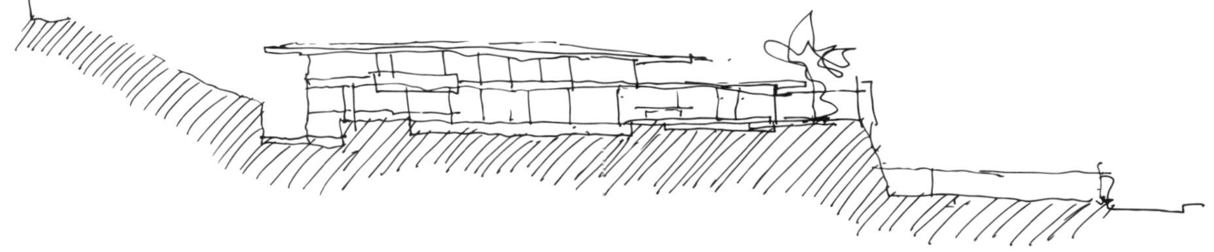

I&L Residence

Block

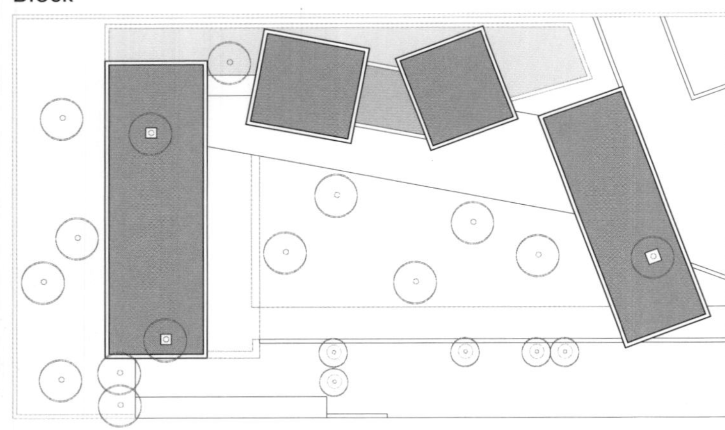

Section

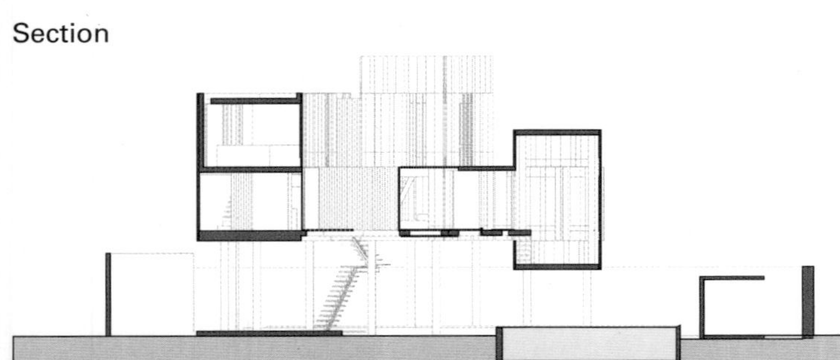

Second Floor

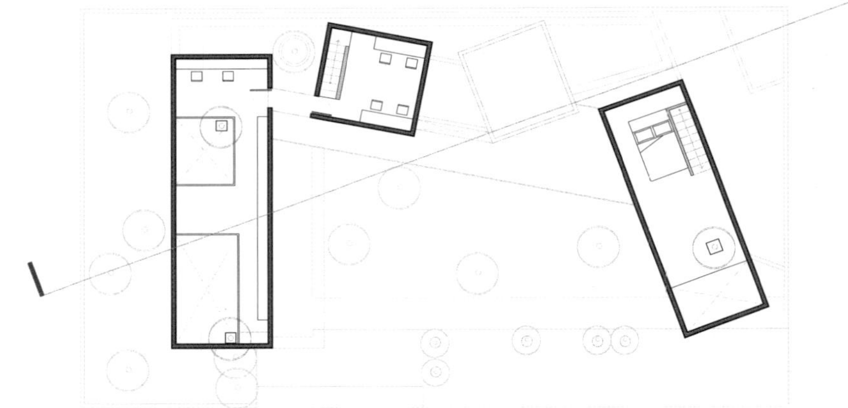

First Floor

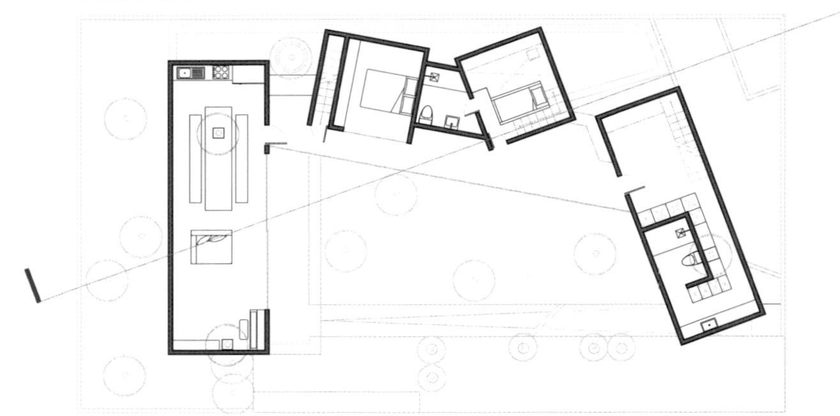

Ground Floor

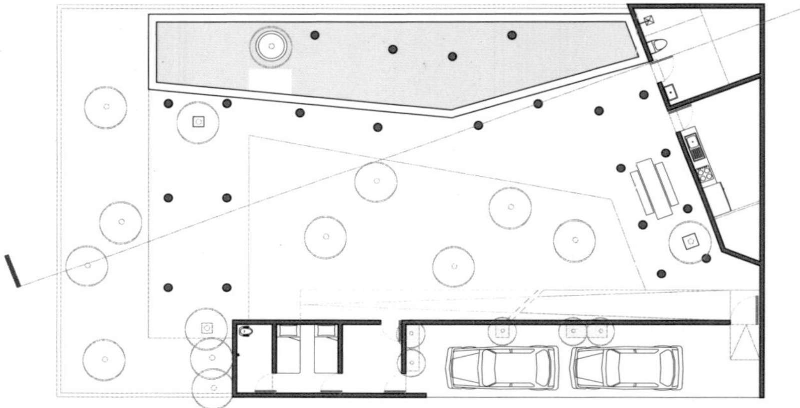

This residence saw Matin employ a deliberate design strategy that embraces a discrepancy between massing orientation and interior space. The building's orientation is straightforward, and the existing tall palm trees have been left intact, utilizing their positions as constraints for laying out the massing. In the space thus delineated, four masses are arranged in an inverted-U composition facing the entrance, with rectangular masses positioned on the left and right sides. In the centre, two squares are located. This arrangement accentuates the courtyard as a vital node for the project.

These masses are interconnected by a long corridor that commences immediately on entering the courtyard. From that point, the floating corridor extends through all the masses, creating a simple yet bold design language. The pilotis seamlessly adapt to the surrounding tall expression of the palm trees, whose influence is significant as they not only provide visual beauty but also shape the spatial ambience of the residence. By incorporating the trees as constraints and aligning the design elements with their graceful presence, the project achieves a cohesive integration of the built environment and the surrounding natural landscape. The palm trees regulate the elements of the house; the branches function as if they are the actual rooftops of the boxes.

Visiting the house offers the experience of being amid floating platform houses, a type of Indonesian vernacular architecture. Each box receives a consistent treatment and expression in terms of materials and facade articulation. Only two dominant materials are apparent — concrete and timber — and the combination of the former's grey hue with the latter's dark tone contributes to the harmonious blend between architecture and nature. Each accommodates a specific programme over its two storeys. For example, in the master bedroom structure, the bathroom is situated on the first floor with the bedroom. To access the library, one must go through the owner's private office.

The site features a distinct rectangular geometry, with the long side facing the street. This architectural characteristic lends a sense of symmetry and balance to the overall design. The straight lines and right angles inherent in the rectangular shape create a structured and organized composition. Additionally, the elongated shape of the site allows for efficient space utilization and facilitates a clear visual connection between the building and its surroundings, as well as providing a solid foundation for the arrangement of the masses and the establishment of spatial relationships.

Spending time in this space brings forth tranquillity and harmony, with the floating platform houses and palm trees establishing a serene and contemplative ambience. The elongated site and deliberate arrangement of masses create a balanced and organized composition that is further enhanced by the floating corridor and the adaptation of the pilotis. These design choices establish a dynamic dialogue between architecture and nature, inviting residents and visitors to immerse themselves in the beauty of the surrounding environment.

NS Residence

Roof

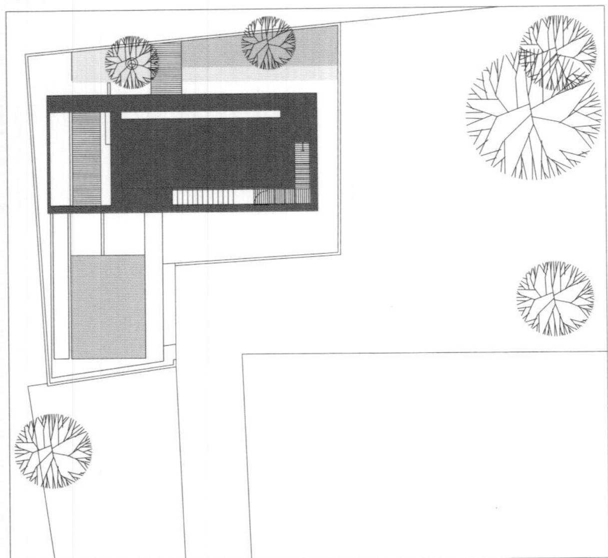

First Floor

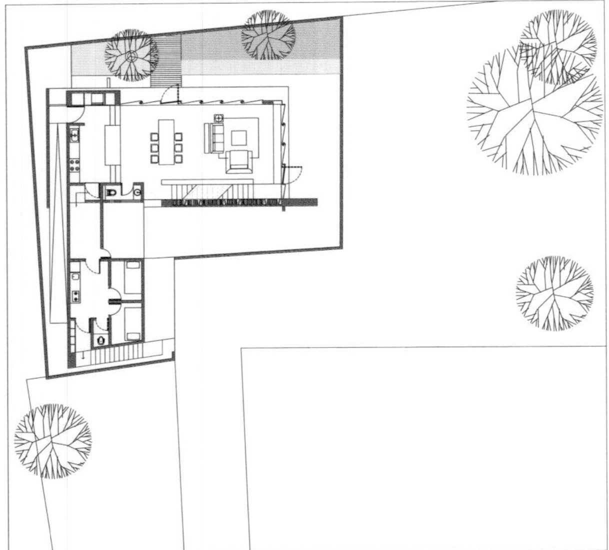

Ground Floor

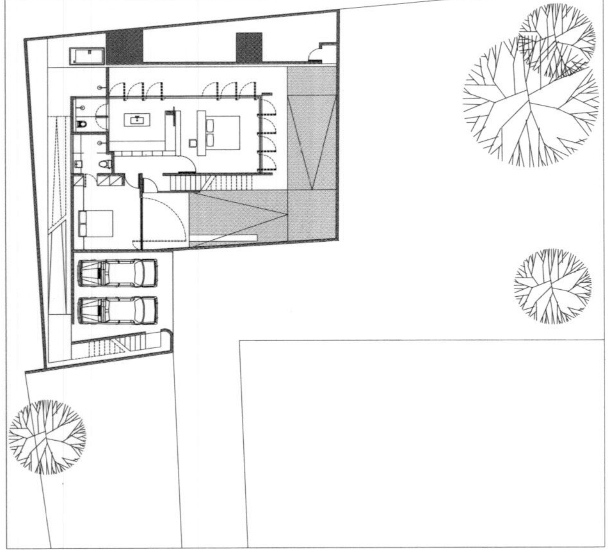

The NS Residence is a two-storey home crafted to cater to the unique requirements of its owner, who works in the country's film industry. Its architectural concept revolves around two primary objectives. Firstly, the owner sought to create a journey-like experience throughout the spaces, while maintaining a subtle yet distinct sense of boundaries. Secondly, given the owner's unpredictable shooting schedule, a key consideration was to provide a resting space that could accommodate an idiosyncratic routine. Consequently, the main bedroom was designed to ensure complete darkness, allowing for uninterrupted rest on returning home.

The house takes on a straightforward L-shaped structure, with the longer, wider side aligned parallel to the east–west axis. The entrance is located on the ground floor, alongside the car park. Moving upstairs leads to the living room, serving as the focal point and the most spacious area.

On entering the living room, visitors are greeted by the presence of a kitchen and access to the servants' spaces. For guests, this marks the culmination of their journey, as the only visible access point beyond is a staircase leading to the rooftop. Enclosed predominantly with glass, the living room creates a floating box-like impression; surrounded by trees, it feels both open and secluded. The architectural configuration, with its high ceiling and cross-ventilation system, also creates a cool microclimate with a relatively low humidity level.

Should the owner or guests desire outdoor activities, options include ascending to the rooftop or relaxing on a small deck situated on the southern side of the living room. This deck provides a cosy space for conversations, enjoying a cup of coffee, reading or simply appreciating the fresh air. The elongated white surface of the deck functions as a canvas for the morning sunlight, and may be the sole vantage point from which visitors can catch a glimpse of the building's facade.

The private chamber, encompassing the owner's bedroom, is located on the ground floor. It can be accessed discreetly through a hidden stairway positioned in the corner opposite the kitchen, which likely remains unnoticed by anyone who has just arrived at the house. The chamber embodies an introverted atmosphere, evoking a cave-like quality. Direct sunlight does not enter the space; instead, soft, diffused light reflects off the surrounding walls and paving throughout the day. If all the openable glass partitions were covered with blackout curtains, not a single ray of light would penetrate the room, fulfilling the owner's desire for complete darkness. The chamber also includes its own bathroom and walk-in closet, effectively functioning as a separate compound and offering that all-important privacy.

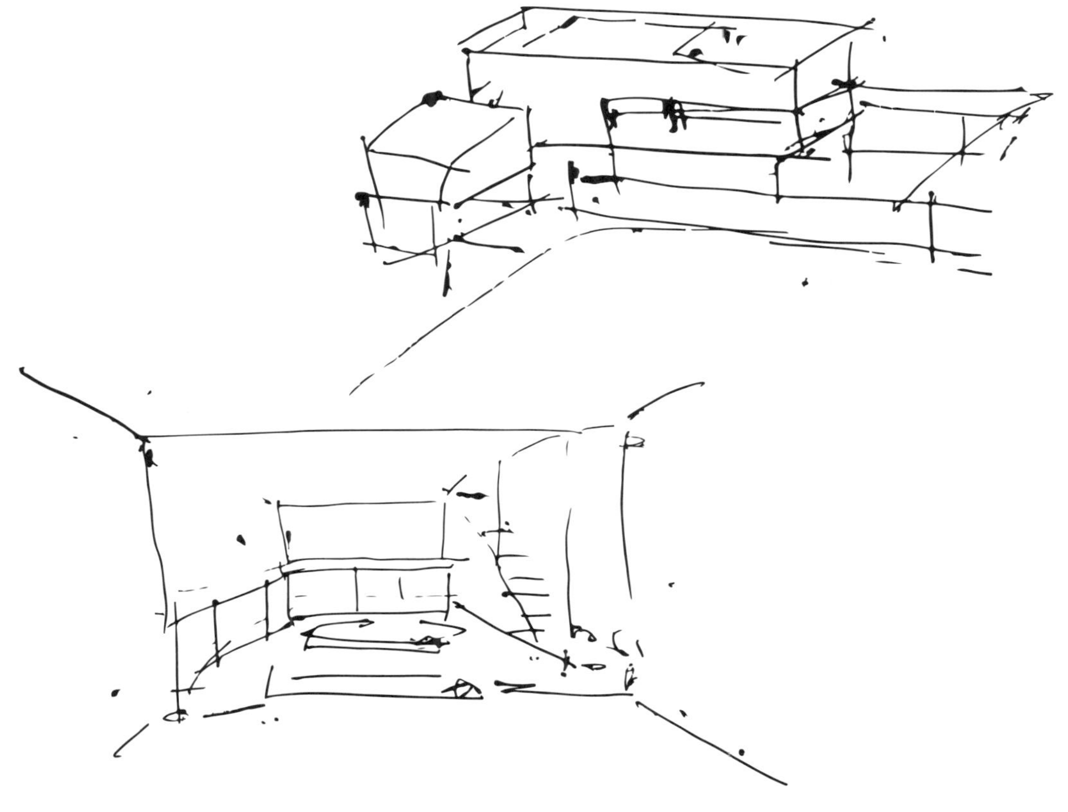

AW Residence

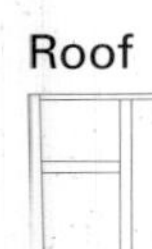

Roof

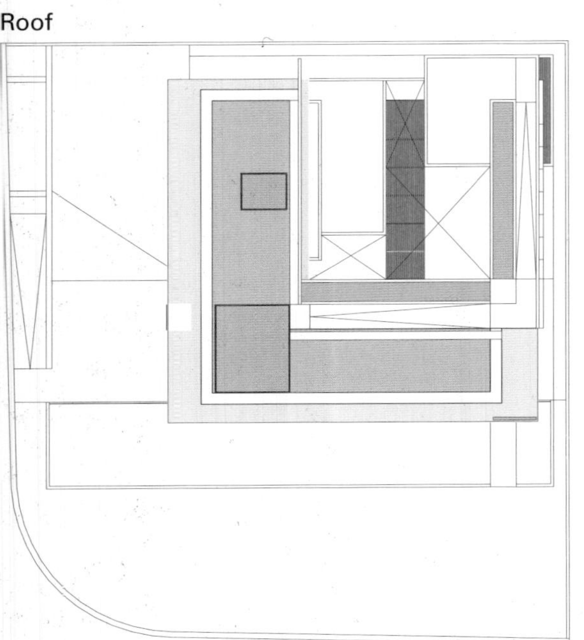

First Floor

Ground Floor

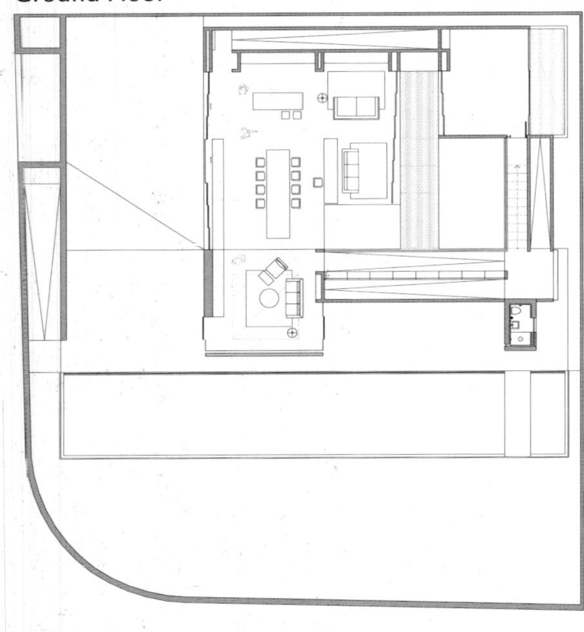

Basement

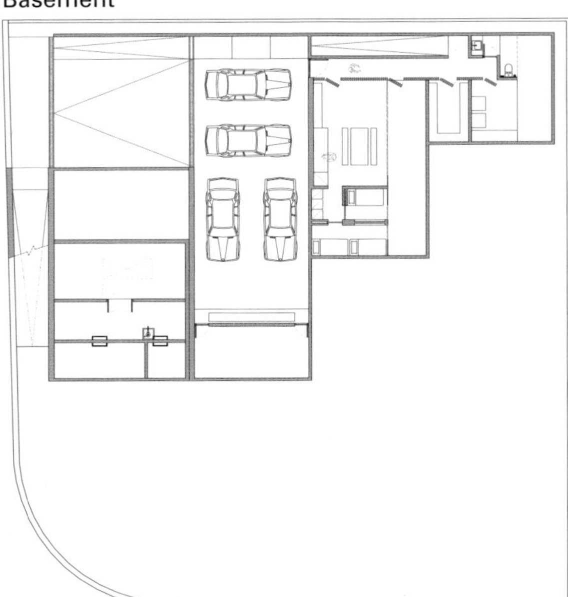

SPICA
GIENAH
24
25

This house in South Jakarta's Cilandak district incorporates three main materials: light concrete walls, black bricks and timber. Concrete predominates in the interior, while the brick walls form the distinctive facade. Timber is utilized for pathways and floors, the whole contributing to the creation of dual personalities: the stacked brick represents the stronger side, evoking the imagery of a castle for the family residing within, while the concrete and timber embody the softer side, imparting a sense of gentleness and warmth.

The building occupies only 50 per cent of the total site area, with the remaining space dedicated to open areas in the form of gardens and terraces. The entrance is positioned on the western side, and a timber-floored pathway leads to the main garden and swimming pool situated on the southern side; the raised garden contours around the house, providing a shield from the noise of the adjacent road. The massing resembles a floating box: there are minimal solid walls on the ground floor, which predominantly features glass partitions that foster a harmonious interplay between the interior and exterior spaces.

Designed as a compound, the house consists of three rectangular boxes arranged in a U-shape, resulting in internal voids. The central courtyard is encompassed by the living room, gym and a ramp leading to the first floor, facilitating a seamless spatial transition from the outdoor swimming pool and garden area to the interior.

One of the notable advantages of incorporating a courtyard, particularly in a tropical climate, is its ability to enhance natural ventilation and establish a favourable microclimate within the house. Here, the courtyard serves as a gateway for refreshing breezes, allowing natural airflow to permeate the living spaces and reducing reliance on air conditioning.

All bedrooms are situated on the first floor, with the main bedroom and bathroom oriented towards the south while the children's bedrooms face west. Adjacent to the children's rooms is a guest room accessible via the same ramp. The basement level is designated for the garage and utility areas.

Designing for a large site can pose challenges, as the scale of architecture can sometimes feel exaggerated. Matin's design strategy for the AW Residence effectively addresses this challenge by using the courtyard to divide the ground floor, creating distinct spaces and mitigating the perception of living in an overly built environment. Each corner of every room establishes a dialogue with the exterior, either opening up to the courtyard or embracing the garden, thus maintaining a strong connection with the surroundings.

Jakarta, 2017

LS Residence

22

Second Floor

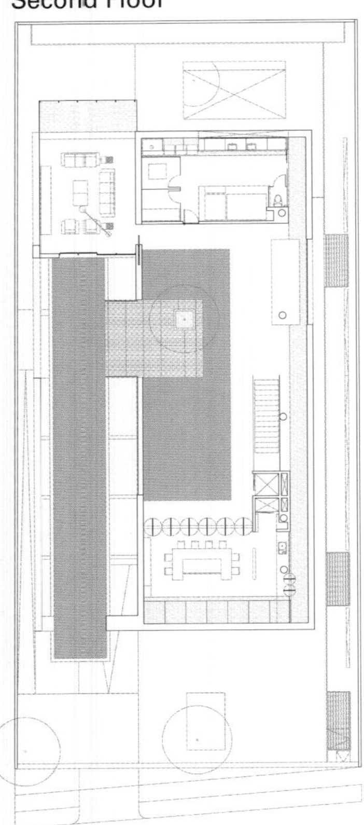

First Floor

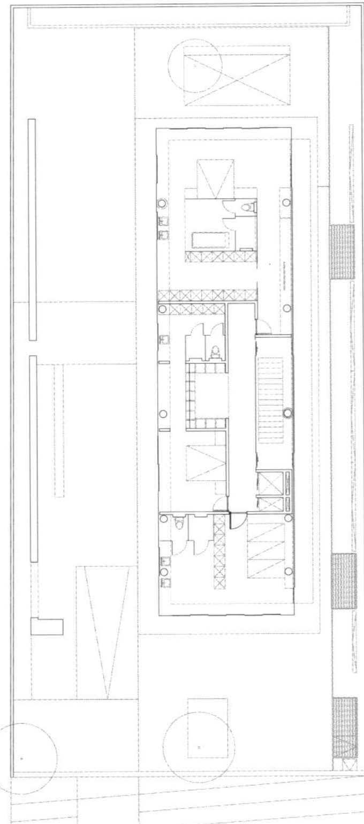

Ground Floor

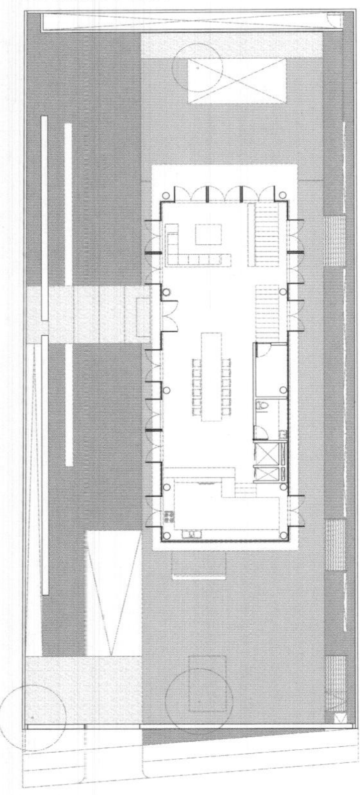

Basement

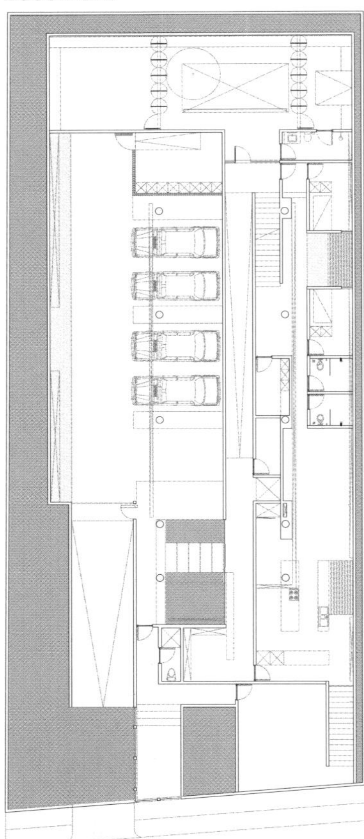

Located in the Menteng area of Central Jakarta, this home accommodates a family with two children. The rectangular lot is divided into two by the north–south axis, with the western side designated for outdoor space. The composition is straightforward, with four storeys stacked vertically in a box.

The house is designed to feel secluded, which becomes evident throughout its circulation and programme zones. The interior–exterior interaction also stands out as a prominent feature in this design, with the facade playing a minimal role. Supported by pilotis, a floating box on the ground floor with a five-metre ceiling height and transparent enclosure establishes an undisturbed view of the scenery, creating a seamless link between the living room and the outside. A waterfall feature on the site's northern wall further enhances the sense of tranquillity.

Approaching the gate, a foyer allows passengers to disembark and their car to proceed to the basement garage. The passengers then access the house through a small corridor behind a thin monumental wall, detached from the structure and enclosing the courtyard on the western side. This courtyard and two ponds at the front and rear encircle the house, blurring the boundaries between the interior and exterior. The ground floor hosts the living room and the main kitchen. The pilotis anchor this level, supporting the box and creating a capacious void that fosters a tranquil living indoor–outdoor space. Notably, the main kitchen is positioned at the front, facing the main gate and functioning as an active space extensively used by the family. A sunken floor in the kitchen area creates an elegant and functional space, smoothly connecting with the front garden pond.

The first floor accommodates three bedrooms, with the main bedroom facing the waterfall feature and the children's bedrooms facing the courtyard and front garden pond respectively. Moving to the second floor, an open outdoor living area awaits. A swimming pool anchors the space, stretching along the western side and accompanied by a bar and pantry that doubles as a lounge on the southern side and another small living–dining area to the north. While these areas draw the eye, the home's basement is not merely a service area but also serves as a functional space, housing a fitness area and a study room for the children.

Matin's final touch is left for the facade, where Corten steel dominates, forming a dark brown oxidation coating that adds a dramatic expression to the simple geometry of the massing.

LH Residence

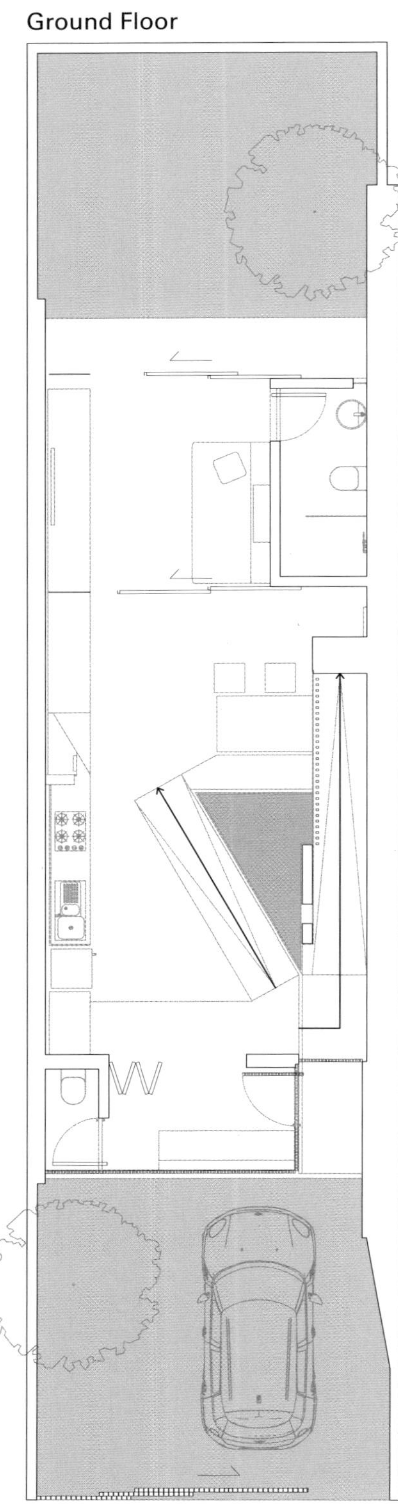
First Floor
Ground Floor
W

The primary challenge of this project lies with the relatively narrow site, enclosed by neighbouring houses in an area of Jakarta where houses are closely adjacent to one another. The house is designed for a small family, necessitating efficiency without compromising spatial comfort.

From the exterior, the house presents itself as an introverted concrete box with few visible openings. However, Matin has masterfully manipulated the interior space to create a dynamic and engaging experience that plays with perceptions. The primary concept behind the design is to enhance linearity, with the strong linear character of the rectangle celebrated and utilized to create a seamless continuous space. To avoid a monotonous environment, which can sometimes occur in a linear space, Matin incorporated floor levels and orientations. Thus, even though the space is linear, the experience within is dynamic: visitors may need to go up, go down or make slight turns, transitioning from narrow spaces to suddenly being welcomed into open areas.

The narrow side of the rectangular site faces the road, and the house's central placement on the site therefore creates two yards: the front yard, which serves as a carport, and the backyard, an extension of the internal living space. Thus, ample space is provided on the ground floor for semi-private activities such as cooking and lounging, while the living room can also be closed by a partition to transform into a guest room for grandparents. The first floor is dedicated to the bedroom, which is the only bedroom in the house, accessible via a ramp along one side of the house that creates a gradual, vertically voluminous connection between the two floors.

On entering the house through a discreet door located at one side, a small foyer is encountered that leads to the main kitchen. The floor level steps down towards the backyard, creating a sense of movement and fluidity in the space.

In an urban setting where green spaces are often scarce, having a backyard becomes even more valuable; here, it not only extends the living space but provides a transition between indoor and outdoor environments, promotes improved air circulation and enhances the indoor air quality. Its health benefits are complemented by a reduced reliance on artificial cooling systems, leading to energy efficiency and cost savings.

A small interruption in the home's centre takes the form of a triangular pond, which acts as a spatial break in the linearity, bringing richness and a point of interest; it effectively transforms the interior into a collection of smaller spaces that interlock with each other from front to back. The void above expands the interior scale, preventing it from feeling cramped or shallow while fostering an intimate connection between the bedroom and the living room. And in conjunction with the greenery outside, it aids air circulation and maintains a comfortable temperature, eliminating the need for a prominent active cooling system.

Omah Jati

Floor Plan

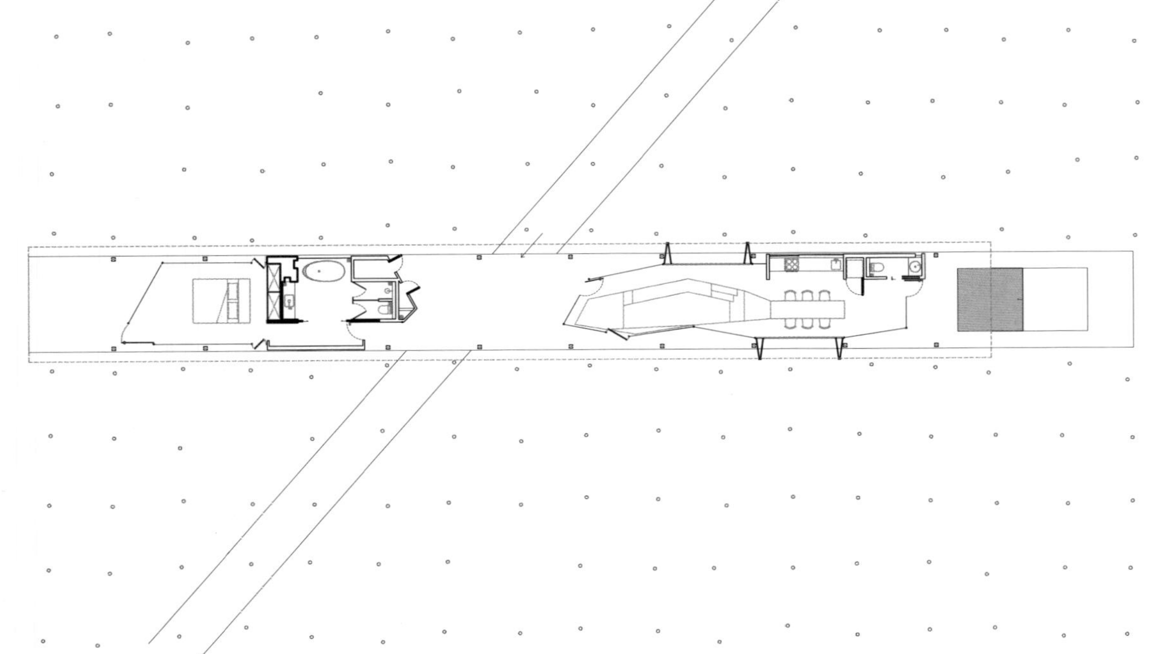

Site Plan

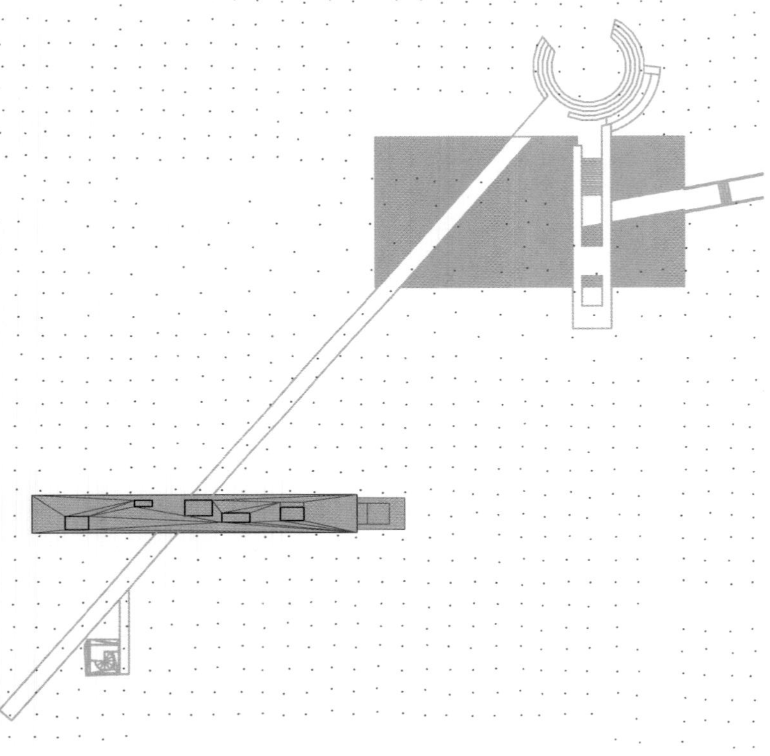

Omah Jati serves as a compelling example of how the natural landscape can greatly enhance the design and aesthetics of a building. Positioned within a three-hectare teak plantation in the western Java area of Banten, the expansive site allows for a thorough exploration of spatial sequences. This approach ensures that visitors are not immediately confronted with the house; instead, it offers them the opportunity to gradually absorb and admire the remarkable natural surroundings, fully immersing themselves in the sublime ambience of the flora.

One of the most noteworthy features of Omah Jati is its adept manipulation of these spatial sequences. Visitors embark on a journey that guides them through various elevations, beginning from the lowest point at the front yard and leading to a cave-like transitional space, ultimately arriving at the central courtyard. It is within this latter space that the house begins to come into view, building anticipation as visitors approach the structure.

Consistent with many of Matin's other works, the ramp takes precedence in welcoming visitors, setting the tone for the entire design. With only three designated areas on the site — an inviting pavilion at the front, an amphitheatre and outdoor gathering space, and the house itself — each element has been crafted with a minimum of materials. The outcome is a streamlined and uncluttered environment, where each programme harmoniously integrates with the forest-like landscape.

The dominant materials throughout are timber for the building and rocks for the pathways and landscape elements. All rocks and stones were sourced from the nearby river and meticulously hand-cut by local artisans, thereby both drawing on local context and supporting heritage craft.

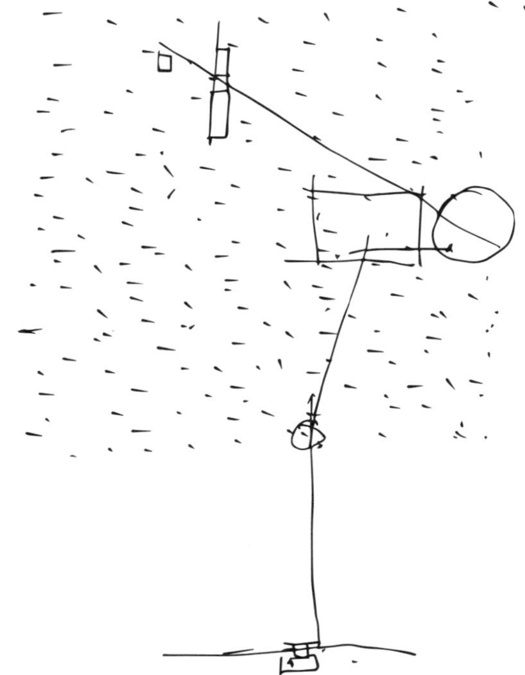

The pathway leading to the house is a timber deck that also links the other architectural features in the amphitheatre and the outdoor gathering space. Serving as the foundation of the design, the pathway creates a cohesive whole that feels both harmonious and organic.

The house itself stands as the focal point of the design: a rectangular structure divided into two sections by a timber deck. The foyer occupies the centre of the structure, allowing visitors to turn left towards the living room or right towards the bedroom. An observation tower, situated at the rear of the house, is also accessible from the foyer.

The living space is a masterpiece, encompassing the main kitchen, a dining area, a sunken living room and an exterior Jacuzzi. Enclosed by glass partitions, the space artfully merges outdoors and indoors, incorporating the teak trees into the interior design. The effect is captivating, creating a sensation of being in direct communion with the natural world.

Equally impressive is the bedroom area, with the main bathroom on one side featuring a centrepiece bathtub that allows complete immersion in the beauty of the forest. The expansive window provides an awe-inspiring tree view, evoking an unparalleled sense of tranquillity and serenity. The main bedroom is located on the opposite side of the bathroom and, though the property is secluded, it can be enclosed with curtains for added privacy.

Climbing the observation tower, made of stone from the river, is an experience in itself, with a robust yet ergonomically designed steel staircase leading visitors to the top. From this vantage point, the view is simply breathtaking: trees extend into the distance, and mountains form a majestic backdrop to the entire scene.

ROCK OPERA
Harry Rush

Y&T Residence

Second Floor

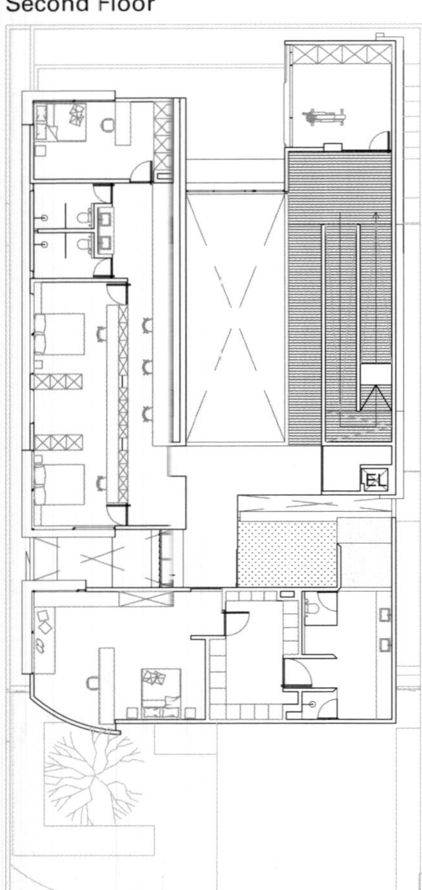

First Floor

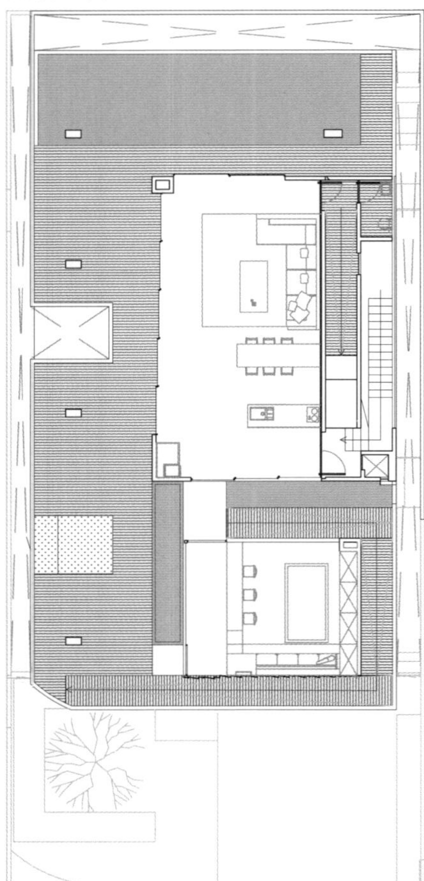

Ground Floor

Nestled within the coastal enclave of Pantai Indah Kapuk in North Jakarta, this four-storey house stands as a testament to Matin's inventive design sensibilities. Departing from his customary architectural approach, the house utilizes a box structure within the confines of a rectangular site while skilfully integrating captivating curvilinear elements. Of particular note, the street-facing facade exudes a subtle yet striking allure, boasting a gentle curve at the corner, heightened by a Corten steel gate and a small parapet crowning the structure. Its raw cement finish profoundly sets the house apart from its surroundings.

On crossing the threshold, the ground floor unfolds as a semi-public domain, designed to extend a warm welcome to guests. Simultaneously, it accommodates a workspace for the family's mother as well as housing the main kitchen — a strategic arrangement to facilitate a seamless ebb and flow of activities. Amid the design directives, the presence of an office on this level remains the sole definitive mandate that guided the house's composition.

Transitioning to the first floor unveils a private library and a generously proportioned living room. The latter, a manifestation of the box geometry, is encircled by glass partitions that fluidly unfurl, blurring the boundaries between indoors and outdoors. This architectural endeavour engenders an expansive, adaptable living milieu, embodying a sense of fluidity and spaciousness that sets the stage for versatile habitation.

The north-oriented expanse of the living area unveils a harmonious interplay between interior and exterior, as a swimming pool establishes an inviting connection. Timber-floored terraces further the sense of informality, culminating in an environment that bridges the interior and exterior seemingly effortlessly. Within the hollow of the box structure, an elegantly arched ceiling takes centre stage, adding a distinctive architectural focal point.

Continuing upwards via a ramp to the second floor reveals the sanctuary of bedrooms, comprising the master bedroom and two children's rooms. The dedication to privacy is paramount: the master, oriented southwards, offers minimal apertures, ensuring a cocooned atmosphere. In contrast, the children's bedrooms, aligned along a corridor, face the central void — a strategic arrangement that introduces a visually engaging effect.

A profound concept — a void within a box — underpins the interior space, orchestrating an orientation that sees all areas converging towards the central void. This design philosophy fosters an introverted ambience steeped in intimacy, prioritizing seclusion and tranquillity. The concept masterfully optimizes spatial allocation, striking an artful equilibrium between openness and enclosure. The central void, emerging as the heart of the dwelling, beckons attention while seamlessly uniting diverse spaces. In this choreographed interplay, natural light permeates deep into the interior, elevating the dance between light and shadow, while the palette of concrete and Corten steel weaves a contemporary yet timeless tapestry.

T Residence & Studio

First Floor

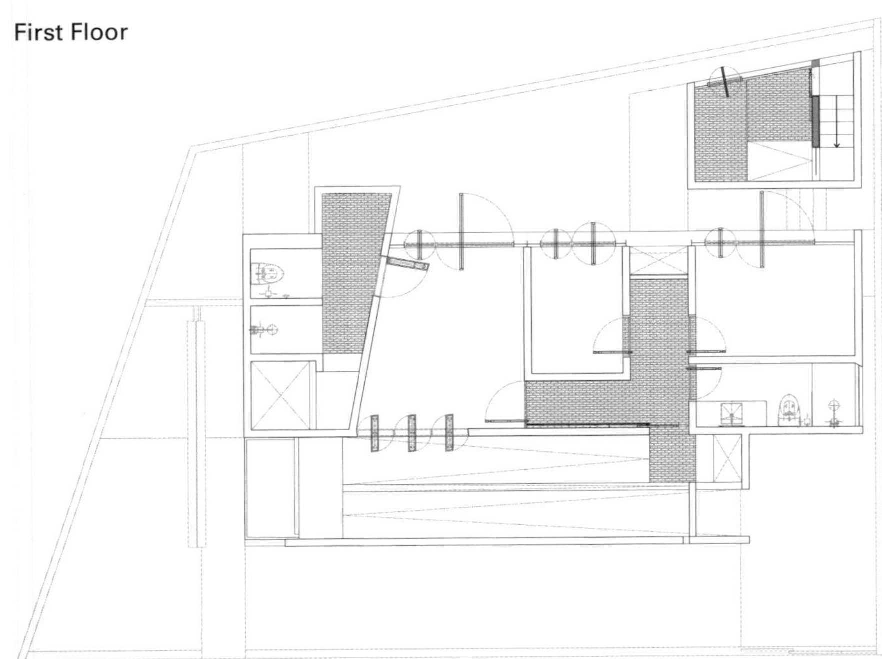

Ground Floor

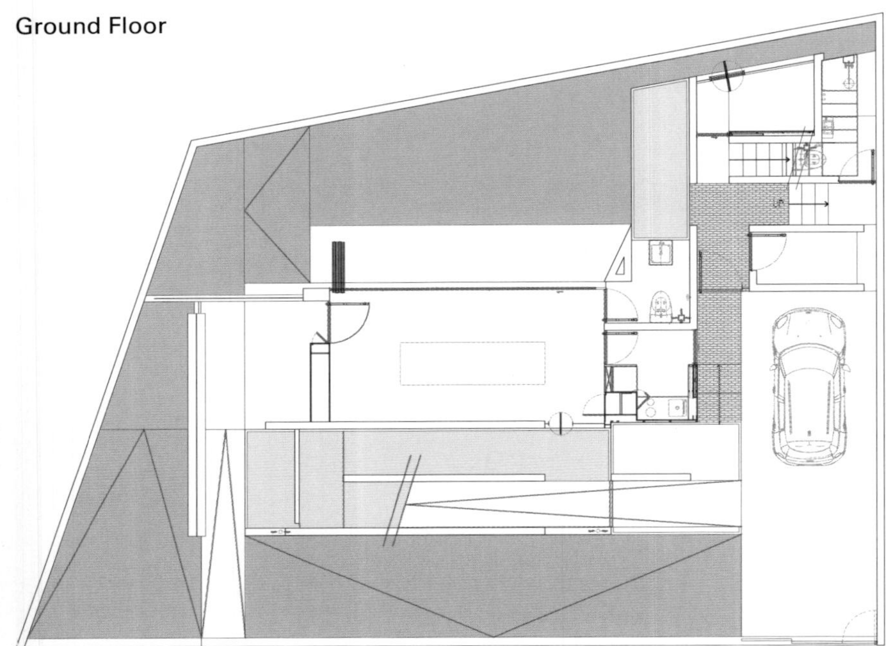

Two elements stand out from a front view of the T Residence & Studio south-west of Jakarta: most apparently, its use of bricks gives it a rustic character that contrasts with its contemporary geometry. Secondly, it appears to have two masses. The main massing serves as the primary residence, while the second massing, located at the back, is utilized as the service area. A corridor connects the two, and links the front yard and backyard. But what makes the house truly unique is the way it utilizes the adjacent narrow site owned by the municipality. While no building can be erected on that land, the design cleverly treats it as an extension of its own green area, giving the house a larger breathing space.

On the ground floor, the main massing features a spacious living room with a sunken dining area that faces the backyard. The space is enclosed with partitions that can be opened to provide flexibility in layout and usage. To access the first floor, a U-shaped ramp is used, which floats above the home's fishpond. Once on the first floor, a corridor is accessed that connects the two wings of the house, one containing the main bedroom and the other a study and small powder room.

One of the prominent features of this design is Matin's thoughtful system of cross-ventilation. Each room has been designed to have sufficient porosity to allow fresh air to circulate and thereby effectively control heat, light and humidity. By strategically incorporating porous elements such as windows, openings and ventilation shafts, the design ensures efficient airflow throughout the house.

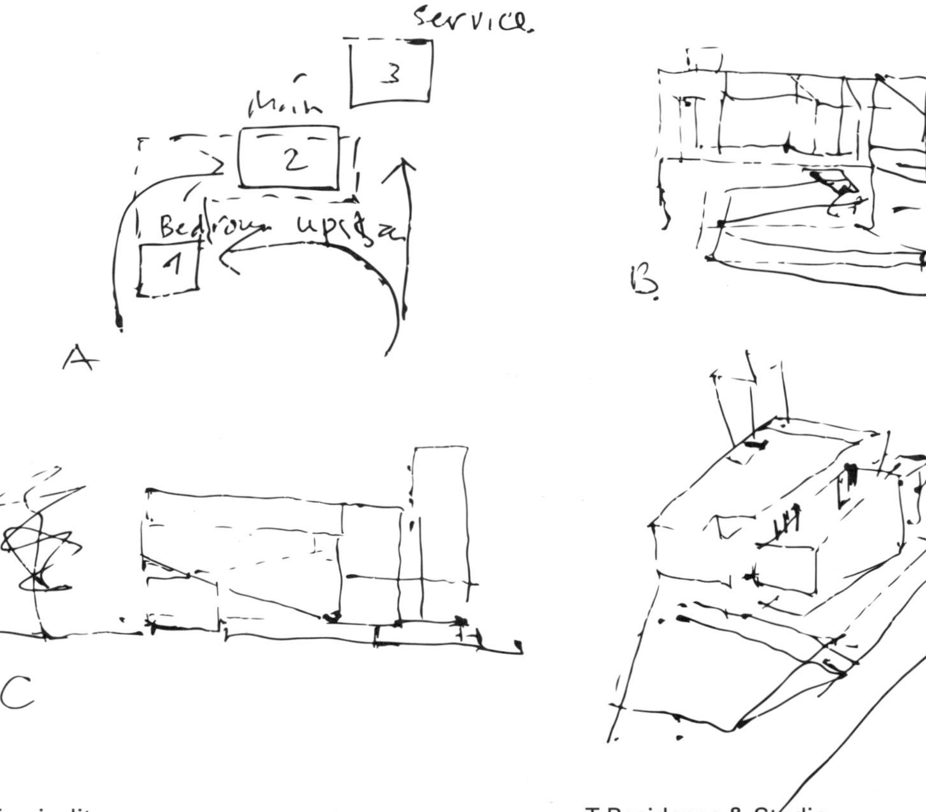

KINFOLK TRAVEL
THE KINFOLK

MA Residence

Roof
Third Floor
Second Floor

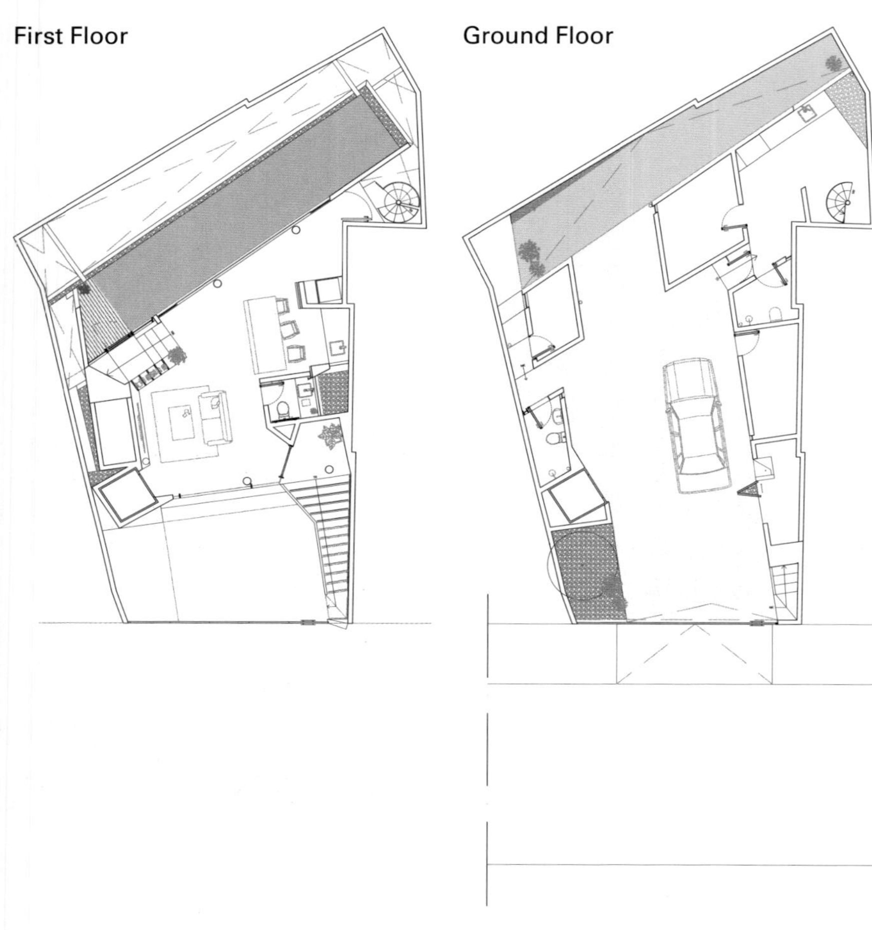
First Floor
Ground Floor

The owner of the MA Residence, a medical practitioner, sought a dwelling that embodied his sense of individuality. Freshly integrated into the urban tapestry of Jakarta's bustling metropolis, this home was to be his bold assertion. Responding adeptly, Matin's muse for the space was the diamond — and much like that stone, the house enraptures and mesmerizes.

The house's massing, composed of triangles rather than a box, adds playfulness to its distinctive design. And among its most arresting attributes, it boasts an exceptional air circulation system and an infusion of abundant natural light — foundational tenets of tropical architecture. To ensure unimpeded airflow, each room features meticulously planned airways to foster cross-ventilation. An ingenious void demarcates the principal bedroom and bathroom on the second floor, channelling both light and air into the welcoming embrace of the first-floor living area. And with Matin ever mindful of maintaining porosity, an air tunnel originating from the roof establishes a conduit to the guest bathroom on the third floor, ensuring both continuous air renewal and a profusion of invigorating natural illumination.

These elements aside, Matin has also crafted a beautiful and functional home despite the lot's compact size, a testament to his refined proficiency in spatial composition. Spread across four storeys, the compact marvel accommodates various programmes, including a swimming pool on the first floor, a master suite on the second floor and three bedrooms on the third floor, with the ground floor home to a garage, helper's room and utility facilities. Vertical movement within the house is made effortless by a small elevator nestled in the garage corner.

Instead of Matin's signature ramp, a small staircase at the northern corner of the ground floor ushers visitors into the first-floor living area. This space is sure to captivate, offering a mesmerizing view of the swimming pool through a long glass partition and exuding serenity and relaxation. A small pantry and toilet add convenience without needing to visit the private floors above.

The MA Residence embodies efficiency, effectiveness and aesthetic value. Emulating the intricacies of origami, the house unfolds a symphony of elements across its plan, while the motif of porosity echoes throughout the volume. Matin's careful orchestration culminates in an extraordinary design that exudes both uniqueness and elegance.

SMEG

PW Villa

Second Floor

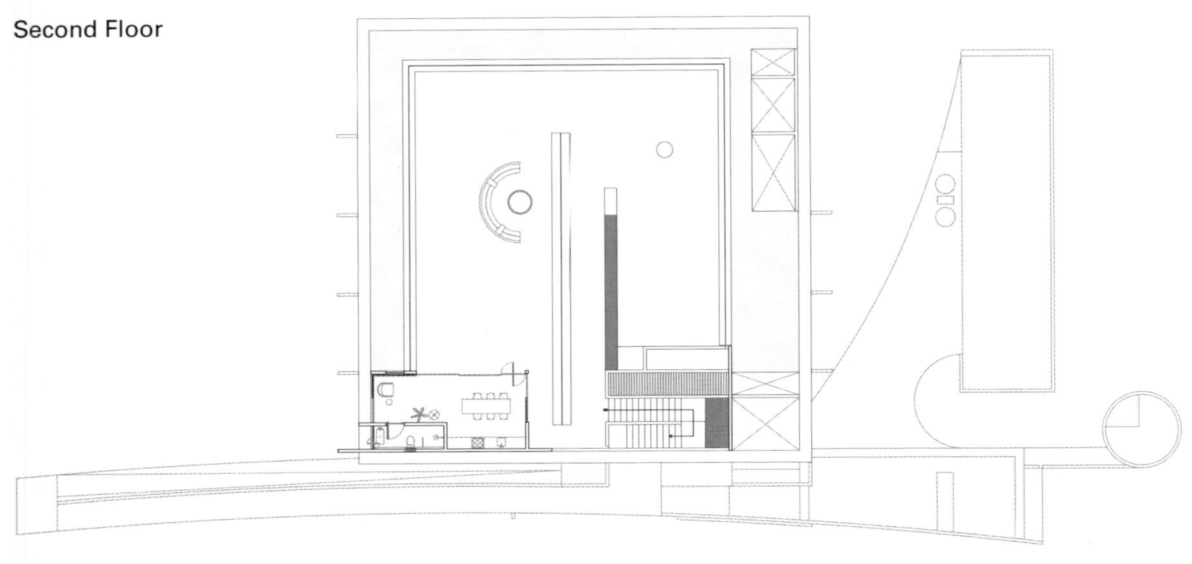

First Floor

Ground Floor

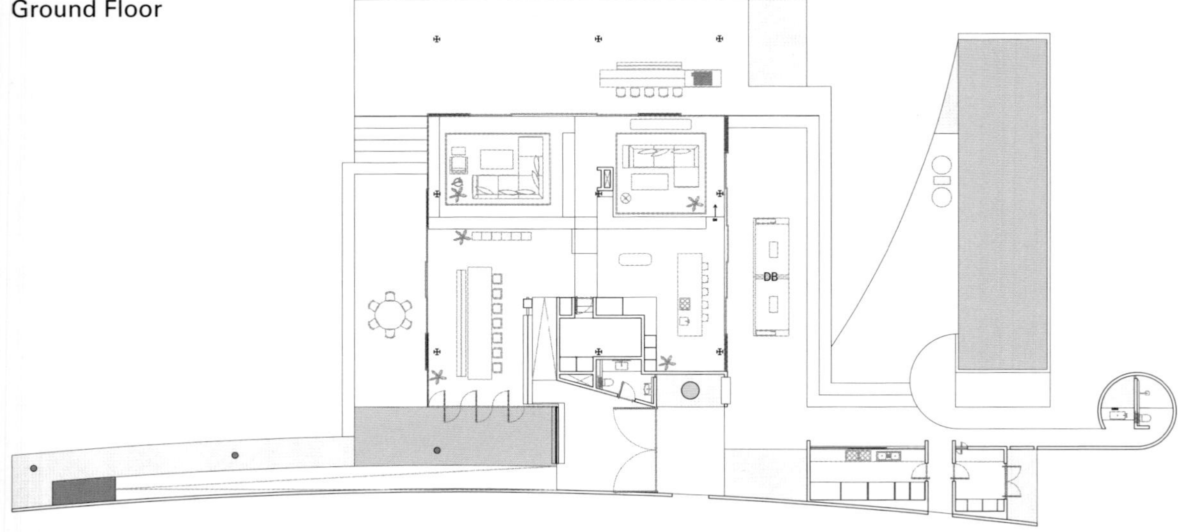

The natural beauty of Cisarua, an enchanting area about 50 kilometres south of Jakarta, provides the perfect backdrop for this exceptional family villa. The inception of the project arose when the owner realized that three majestic mountains in West Java — Salak, Pangrango and Gede — were visible from his four-hectare property. This realization ignited the idea of creating an elevated space that allowed him to fully immerse himself in this extraordinary view, in turn prompting him to demolish his existing villa and reconstruct it so as to fully embrace the site's potential.

As a result, the primary focus of the design brief was to establish that strategic vantage point. The owner also holds an affinity for terraces, and desired terraces in the new house reminiscent of those in the former villa.

On entering the compound, the villa immediately captures attention as the main attraction. A floating concrete box perched atop the property's highest point offers an unobstructed vista of the entire area. The ground floor is enveloped by glass doors connecting the interior and exterior spaces, while the first floor, which accommodates the bedrooms, is enclosed in concrete, symbolizing the villa's private realm.

One of the home's most distinctive attributes is its departure from the conventional front facade. Instead, the side facing the parking area presents a flat concrete surface with a small opening at the top, cultivating an attitude of reverence and humility towards the surrounding natural beauty. But rather than pushing visitors away, this design element sparks curiosity and inspires further exploration.

The alluring exterior is characterized by clean lines and a simple composition and geometry. On entering the parking area, a grand vase extends a welcoming gesture, heralding the elegance and sophistication that await. The outdoor area with its swimming pool connects to and seems to encompass the primary kitchen, providing an inviting expanse for entertaining and relaxation.

Once indoors, a ramp corridor guides visitors to the inviting living spaces. Expansive openings on two sides of the main living room offer breathtaking views of the surroundings, fostering an atmosphere of serenity and a connection with nature. Moving to the first floor reveals the bedroom section, comprising a master bedroom and several guest rooms. Thoughtfully arranged along a central corridor and with each having its own bathroom, the rooms are designed for guests' privacy and comfort.

The balconies attached to each guest room are standout features, including bathtubs where guests can luxuriate in the fresh air and captivating scenery. Meanwhile, at the end of the corridor, the master bedroom offers a private and lavish retreat — an ideal sanctuary for unwinding and savouring the stunning vistas.

At the very top, the roof deck not only fulfils the owner's desire for panoramic mountain views, but offers a capacious platform for hosting outdoor gatherings. This open-air terrace allows guests to embrace the grandeur of nature and momentarily detach from the pace of Jakarta's cosmopolitan life; it's a place where the serene ambience and awe-inspiring panoramas create a rejuvenating experience that leaves an indelible imprint.

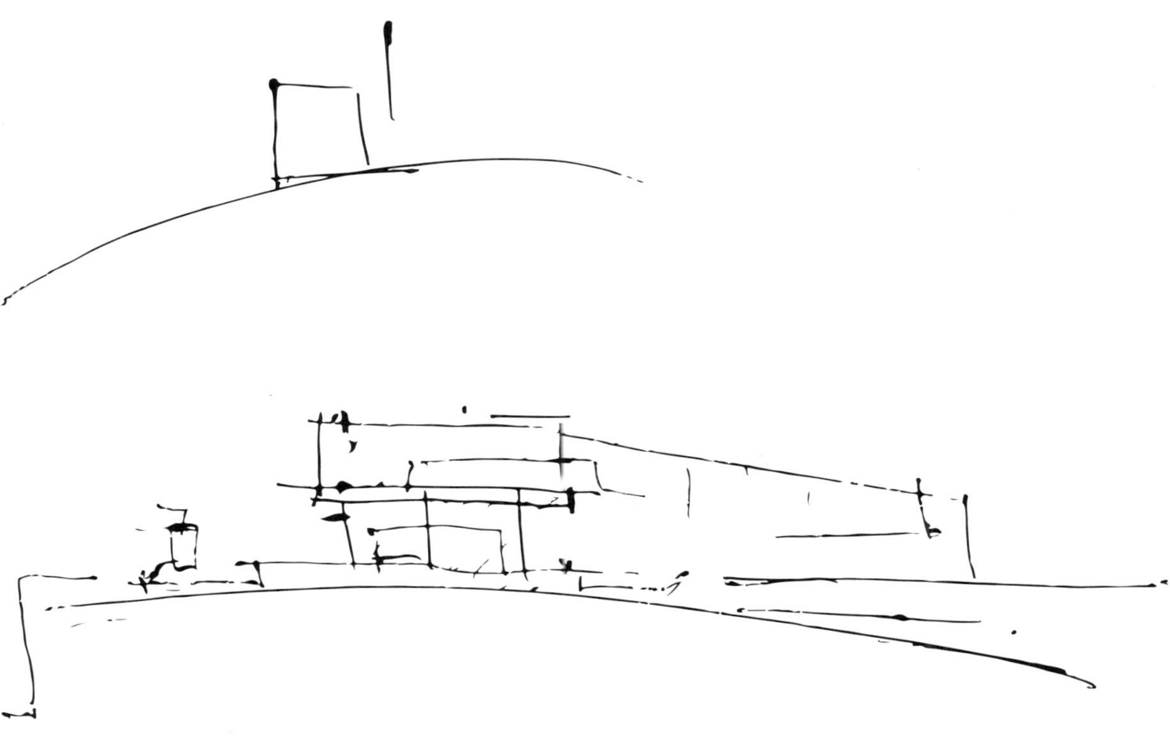

Andra Matin

Profile

Biography

Name
Isandra Matin Ahmad (Andra Matin)

Born
Bandung, Indonesia, August 1962

Lives & works
Jakarta, Indonesia

Education
Parahyangan Catholic University, Bandung, 1981

Website
andramatin.com

Selected Works

2023
Roemah Koffie, Bali
Pignatelli Triputra University, Surakarta

2022
Lokananta Revitalization, Surakarta

2021
Pepper Plantation, Belitung
Srihadi Soedarsono Museum, Bandung

2020
Alun-Alun Kediri, Kediri
ARTOTEL Cabin Bromo, Probolinggo

2019
Masjid Apung Ancol, Jakarta
Revitalization of Taman Ismail Marzuki Cultural Centre, Jakarta

2018
Aquatic Stadium Gelora Bung Karno, Jakarta
Syech Yusuf Discovery Park, Makassar

2017
Titik Dua Hotel, Bali
GGF Development, Terbanggi Besar

2016
As Sobur Mosque & Function Room, Tulang Bawang Barat
Cork & Screw Country Club, Jakarta

2015
ARTOTEL Gajahmada, Semarang

2014
International Airport, Banyuwangi
Secret Garden Village, Bali

2013
AD Premier Office Building, Jakarta

2012
Redesign of Vida Bekasi Masterplan, West Java
AM Residence, Jakarta

2010
Katamama Hotel, Bali
Potato Head Beach Club, Bali

2007
Deltomed Office, Tawangmangu

2006
Tanah Teduh Compound, Jakarta
WH Residence, Jakarta

2000
Gedung Dua8 Museum, Jakarta

1999
Le Bo Ye Graphic Design Office, Jakarta

Awards

2022
Winner, Aga Khan Award for Architecture
Banyuwangi International Airport

2021
Winner, Design Anthology Awards (Architect Category)

2020
Winner, IAI Jakarta Awards (Conservation Category)
Aquatic Stadium Gelora Bung Karno, Jakarta

2020
Winner, INDE.Awards (The Luminary Category)

2019–20
Shortlisted, Aga Khan Award for Architecture
AM Residence

2018
Special Mention, 16th Venice Architecture Biennale
Elevation

2012
Winner, IAI Jakarta Awards (Special Category)
Komunitas Salihara (collaboration with Adi Purnomo and Marco Kusumawijaya)

2008
Winner, IAI Jakarta Awards
Infinity Wedding Chapel, Conrad Bali (in collaboration with Antony Liu)

2006
Winner, National IAI Award, Winfred Hutabarat Residence
Winner, National IAI Award, Javaplant Office

2002
Citation, National IAI Award
Gedung Dua8 Museum

1999
Winner, National IAI Award (Commercial Building)
Le Bo Ye Graphic Design Office

Competitions

2019
1st Prize, Terminal 4 Soekarno-Hatta International Airport, Jakarta

2007
1st Prize, Revitalization of Taman Ismail Marzuki Cultural Centre, Jakarta

Public Lectures & Discussions

2023
Keynote Speaker, Aga Khan Award for Architecture, Singapore University of Technology and Design, Singapore

2021
Keynote Speaker, UIA 2021 Rio 27th World Congress of Architects, Rio de Janeiro

2020
Anthology Architecture & Design Festival, Manila

2019
ARCASIA Forum, Dhaka
Tokyo Institute of Technology
Archi-Depot, Tokyo

2018
16th Venice Architecture Biennale: Meetings On Architecture
AIA, Singapore
ETH Zurich
MASA Annual Event, Bangalore

2016
IIA Cochin Centre, India
House Vision, Tokyo

2015
Bengal Institute for Architecture, Landscapes and Settlements, Dhaka

2014
China Academy of Art, Hangzhou
University of Melbourne

Exhibitions

2023
Local Airport Design Workshop, Aga Khan Award for Architecture Event 2023, Banyuwangi, Indonesia

2019
Prihal: arsitektur andramatin Solo Exhibition, Jakarta
Archifest, Singapore
100 Experiments, Aedes Architecture Forum, Berlin
Green, Green and Tropical — Woodified Architecture in Southeast Asia, Tokyo

2018
16th Venice Architecture Biennale

2017
Maison&Objet, Paris

2016
RUMAH ('House') Solo Exhibition, Jakarta
Indonesialand Architecture Festival, Bandung

2015
Tropicality: Revisited — Recent Approaches by Indonesian Architects, Deutsches Architekturmuseum, Frankfurt

2014
14th Venice Architecture Biennale, Venice

2012
Andra Matin: Sebuah Sekuel Solo Exhibition, Jakarta

2011
Architecture Biennale Rotterdam

Publications

Visionary Architects of Monsoon Asia
atelier international, 2023

The Brutalists
Phaidon, 2023

GA Houses
Issue 187, March 2023

Inclusive Architecture: Aga Khan Award for Architecture
2022

The Monocle Book of Homes
Monocle, 2021

Domus
Interview with David Chipperfield, March 2020

Architectural Review Asia Pacific
Issue 166, 2020

台灣建築 (*Taiwan Architecture*)
Issue 298, July 2020

Tropical Architecture for the 21st Century
BluPrint, 2019

Courtyard Living: Contemporary Houses of the Asia-Pacific
Thames & Hudson, 2019

Design Anthology
Issue 18, September 2018

Archinesia
Issue 13, May 2018

Design Anthology
Issue 9, June 2016

a+u Architecture and Urbanism
Special issue, May 2016

GA Masterpieces 2001–2015
2016

Monocle
March 2016

Habitus
Issue 24, July–September 2014

GA Houses
Issue 138, July 2014

Mark
Issue 44, June–July 2013

The Phaidon Atlas of 21st Century World Architecture
Phaidon, 2008

The Wallpaper* Architects Directory
2007

New Directions in Tropical Asian Architecture
Periplus Editions, 2005

Project Credits

WH Residence

Location
Jakarta

Design
2002–2003

Construction
2004–2006

Principal
Andra Matin

Architecture team
Avianti Armand, Astrid Susanti, Daliana Suryawinata, Ranidia Leeman, Meidy Suriansyah, Heddy Purnomo, Iboy Sulaeman

Interior team
Avianti Armand, Astrid Susanti, Prodak team

Structural engineer
Davy Sukamta & Partners

Mechanical engineer
Maksudi

Landscape
Lia Hasibuan

General contractor
Alex Gandung

IT Residence

Location
Bogor

Design
2009–2010

Construction
2010–2012

Principal
Andra Matin

Architecture team
Ady Putra Sanjaya, Agatha Carolina, Suhaedi

Structural engineer
Hermanto Subagijo

Mechanical engineer
Danol Adam

Landscape
Andra Matin

General contractor
Bebeng & NAD

AM Residence

Location
Jakarta

Design
2008–2010

Construction
2008–2012

Principal
Andra Matin

Architecture team
Asep Tatang, Misandi Jaya, Heddy Purnomo

Interior team
Andra Matin, Audite Matin

Structural engineer
Alex Gandung

Mechanical engineer
Alex Gandung

Landscape
Andra Matin

General contractor
Alex Gandung

AS Residence

Location
Yogyakarta

Design
2009–2010

Construction
2010–2013

Principal
Andra Matin

Architecture team
Titis Nurabadi, Tommy Sandjaja, Misandi Jaya, Suhaedi

Structural engineer
Melanie

Mechanical engineer
Johanes Medijana

Landscape
andramatin

Lighting designer
Iskandar Loedin

General contractor
Johanes Medijana

EH Residence

Location
Bandung

Design
2009–2010

Construction
2011–2013

Principal
Andra Matin

Architecture team
Patisandhika Sidarta, Yogi Ferdinand, Fandy Gunawan, Erick VH, Suhaedi

Interior team
andramatin & owner

Structural engineer
HEPSA Consultant

Mechanical engineer
Basuki Terliatan

Landscape
andramatin

General contractor
Basuki Terliatan

I&L Residence

Location
Jakarta

Design
2000–2001, 2013–2015

Construction
2013–2015

Principal
Andra Matin

Architecture team
Ady Putra Sanjaya, Gana Ganesha, Suhaedi

Structural engineer
Hadi Jahja & Associates

Mechanical engineer
Alex Gandung

General contractor
Alex Gandung

AW Residence

Location
Jakarta

Design
2011–2012

Construction
2013–2017

Principal
Andra Matin

Architecture team
Yogi Ferdinand, Chrisye Octaviani, Fauzia Evanindya, Suhaedi

Interior team
Ethelind Laurencia, Asep Tatang

Structural engineer
Hadi Jahja & Associates

Mechanical engineer
Tritunggal Global Mahakarya

Landscape
Andra Matin

Lighting Designer
Hadi Komara

General contractor
Dwitunggal Mandirijaya

LH Residence

Location
Jakarta

Design
2013–2014

Construction
2016–2018

Principal
Andra Matin

Architecture team
Astrid Susanti

Structural engineer
Alex Gandung

Mechanical engineer
Alex Gandung

General contractor
Alex Gandung

Y&T Residence

Location
Jakarta

Design
2017–2018

Construction
2019–2022

Principal
Andra Matin

Architecture team
Gana Ganesha, Jonathan Raditya, Matthew Groversam

Interior team
Paramayuda Maulana

Structural engineer
Hadi Jahja & Associates

Mechanical engineer
Rusman Riadi

Landscape
Plantyourplan

General contractor
Pipih Priyatna

MA Residence

Location
Jakarta

Design
2020

Construction
2020–2022

Principal
Andra Matin

Project team (architecture & interior)
Martinus Anton Setyadji, Aistyara Charmita, Dicky Huang, Brusli

Structural engineer
Mohamad Samsi

Mechanical engineer
Mohamad Samsi

General contractor
Mohamad Samsi

IH Residence

Location
Bandung

Design
2006–2007, 2012–2013

Construction
2013–2015

Principal
Andra Matin

Architecture team
Wiyoga Nurdiansyah, Dhanie Syawaliah, Suhaedi

Interior team
Audite Matin, Ethelind Laurencia

Structural engineer
Djulianto Hadimuljo

Mechanical engineer
Hanny Kon

Landscape
Ruang Hijau

General contractor
Indra Santoso Kartika

NS Residence

Location
Jakarta

Design
2012–2013

Construction
2013–2015

Principal
Andra Matin

Architecture team
Ady Putra Sanjaya, Sandro Devriadi, Suhaedi

Structural engineer
Hadi Jahja & Associates

Mechanical engineer
Alex Gandung

General contractor
Alex Gandung

LS Residence

Location
Jakarta

Design
2011–2012

Construction
2013–2017

Principal
Andra Matin

Architecture team
Yogi Ferdinand, Asep Tatang, Suhaedi

Structural engineer
Hadi Jahja & Associates

Mechanical engineer
Tritunggal Global Mahakarya

Landscape
Andra Matin

Lighting Designer
Hadi Komara

General contractor
Dwitunggal Mandirijaya

Omah Jati

Location
Banten

Design
2017–2018

Construction
2018–2021

Principal
Andra Matin

Architecture team
Natasha Astari, Sandro Devriadi, Sovie Khuswa, Suhaedi

Interior team
Paramayuda Maulana, Audite Matin

Structural engineer
Baskara & Woodlam

Mechanical engineer
Satya Karya Prima

General contractor
Satya Karya Prima

T Residence & Studio

Location
Tangerang Selatan

Design
2019

Construction
2019–2022

Principal
Andra Matin

Architecture team
Ephraem Joseph, Bernardus Rosario

Structural engineer
Advicon

Mechanical engineer
Advicon

General contractor
Advicon

PW Villa

Location
Cisarua

Design
2021

Construction
2021–2023

Principal
Andra Matin

Architecture team
Akhyar Maulidan, Matthew Groversam

Interior team
Stella Thamrin, Brusli, Ceria Justianto

Structural engineer
PT. Bangun Utama

Mechanical engineer
PT. Bangun Utama

General contractor
PT. Bangun Utama

Project Editor
Suzy Annetta

Content Editor
Philip Annetta

Art Director
Jeremy Smart

Photographer
Davy Linggar

Writers
David Hutama
Lyndon Neri

andramatin Team
Angie Miranti
Fakhrell Saqfan Izzan

Wonders of Weaving
Yenny Gunawan

Special Thanks
Lim Masulin

David Hutama
David Hutama is an architecture writer and educator who is deeply committed to the advancement of innovative pedagogy in design and architecture. His approach privileges a thorough understanding of historical knowledge and theoretical frameworks, which provide an experimental landscape spanning the entirety of human civilization.

Hutama is a PhD supervisor at Ghent University and a visiting lecturer at Pelita Harapan University, as well as co-founder of Nenun Ruang, an educational hub dedicated to architecture, design and craft. He received his PhD from the AA School, in addition to holding a Master of Engineering, Architectural History and Criticism from Toyohashi University of Technology and a Bachelor of Architecture from Parahyangan Catholic University.

Lyndon Neri
Lyndon Neri co-founded Neri&Hu Design and Research Office with Rossana Hu in 2006; the interdisciplinary architectural design practice is based in Shanghai, with satellite offices in Milan and Paris. Neri received his Master of Architecture at Harvard Graduate School of Design and his Bachelor of Arts in Architecture at University of California, Berkeley.

Neri has been deeply committed to architectural education throughout his career. He was appointed Visiting Faculty at Princeton University School of Architecture in 2024, Howard Friedman Visiting Professor of Practice at University of California, Berkeley in 2023, Design Critic in 2023 and John C. Portman Design Critic in Architecture in 2019 and 2021 at Harvard Graduate School of Design, and Eero Saarinen Visiting Professor in 2022 and Norman R. Foster Visiting Professor Chair in 2018 at Yale School of Architecture.

Davy Linggar
Davy Linggar is a multidisciplinary artist based in Jakarta who works primarily through the mediums of photography and painting. There is a substantial breadth to his practice in his investigation of the things that constitute an image and its interrelatedness to perception, memory, form, feeling and experience. His acute sensibilities are then translated into a diverse array of possibilities – be it through moving images, photographs, paintings or drawings.

In establishing a distinctive aesthetic vernacular, Linggar engages with and through architecture, popular culture, fashion and nature. He deftly negotiates and finds balance between many different forms of energy and forces. Linggar is also a Leica Ambassador to Indonesia, as well as a Visiting Professor at the University of Indonesia (Universitas Indonesia).

On the front cover:
The semi-open living space of the AM Residence in South Jakarta, which is exemplary of Andra Matin's contemporary approach to architecture in tropical climates (page 26)

On the back cover, clockwise from top left:
Omah Jati in western Java (page 170); the IT Residence in Bogor (page 44); the Y&T Residence in North Jakarta (page 190); the I&L residence in Jakarta (page 102); the IT Residence; the AM Residence

First published in the United Kingdom in 2024 by
Thames & Hudson Ltd, 181A High Holborn, London WC1V 7QX

First published in the United States of America in 2024 by
Thames & Hudson Inc., 500 Fifth Avenue, New York, New York 10110

British Library Cataloguing-in-Publication Data
A catalogue record for this book is available from the British Library

Library of Congress Control Number 2024932556

ISBN 978-0-500-34375-3

Printed in China by RR Donnelley

Produced with the support of Wonders of Weaving